SUPERHEROES

INSPIRING STORIES
of SECRET STRENGTH

Illustrated by Denzell Dankwah

SOPHIA THAKUR
with an introduction by STORMZY

Penguin Random House UK

Words by Sophia Thakur
Illustrations by Denzell Dankwah
Cover Design by Emma Grey Gelder
Cover Lettering by Kate Forrester
Layout and Typography by Andreas Brooks

First published by #Merky Books in 2021

www.penguin.co.uk

A CIP catalogue record for this book is available from the British Library.
ISBN 9781529118896

Printed and bound by Firmengruppe APPL, aprinta druck GmbH, Wemding, Germany

The authorised representative in the EEA is Penguin Random House Ireland, Morrison Chambers, 32 Nassau Street, Dublin D02 YH68.

Penguin Random House is committed to a sustainable future for our business, our readers and our planet. This book is made from Forest Stewardship Council® certified paper.

FSC www.fsc.org MIX Paper from responsible sources FSC® C018179

#Merky Books
20 Vauxhall Bridge Road
London SW1V 2SA

#Merky Books is part of the Penguin Random House group of companies whose addresses can be found at global.penguinrandomhouse.com.

THIS BOOK BELONGS TO

....

CONTENTS

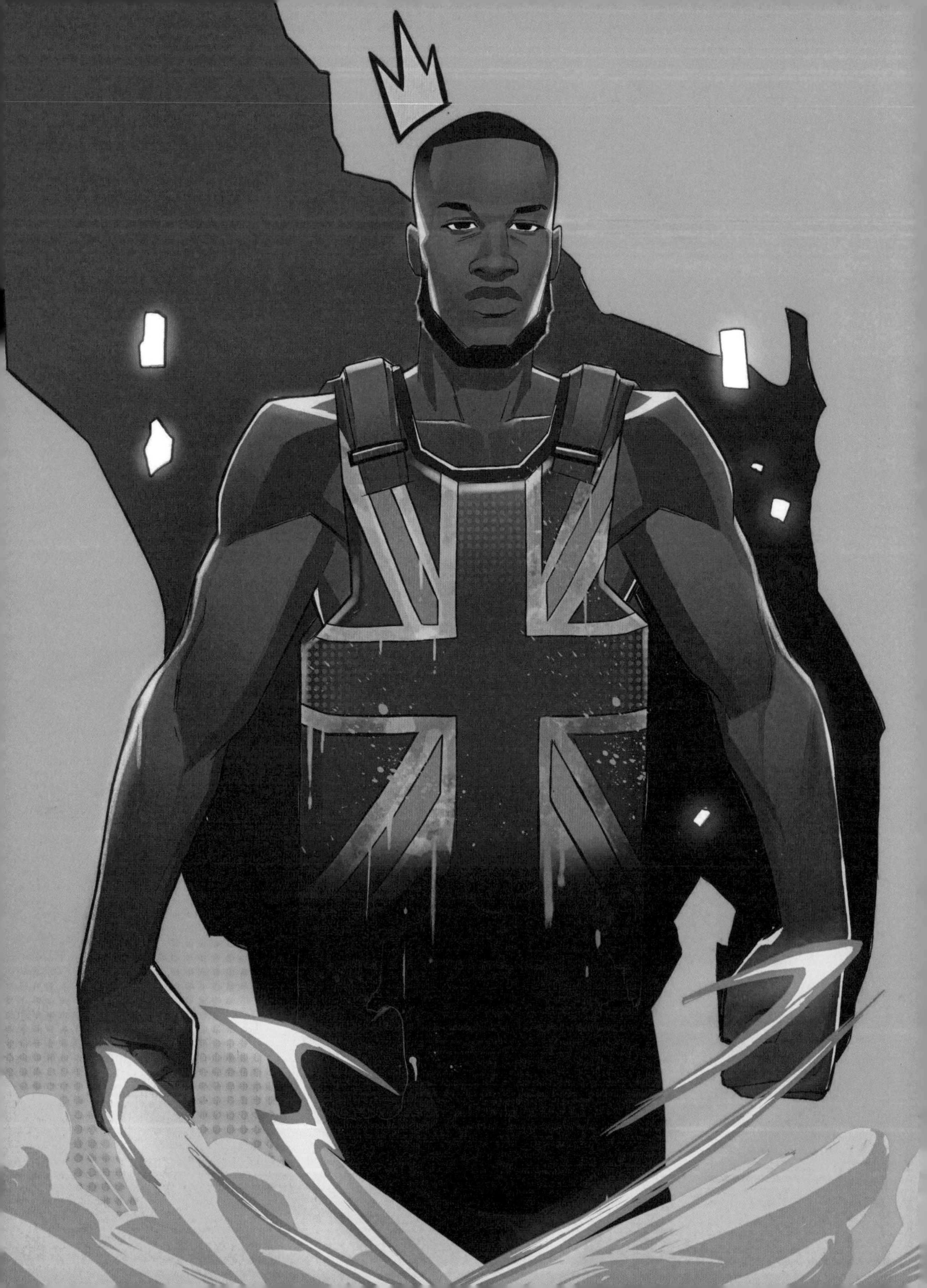

When I was younger, I used to MC in the school playground and in my local area, spitting with my friends and telling stories. Music has always been a huge part of my life, but at the time, I didn't understand that it was a talent — that it was my superpower and it made me unique.

Growing up in South London as a young Black man from an underprivileged background, there weren't many role models that I could aspire to be like. There came a moment when that changed, and when I realised that I could turn my superpower into something extraordinary. I was at home watching Channel U and saw other people that looked like me — artists making waves in the music scene and being successful. It was then that I was inspired to start my own journey.

I want this book to be for you what the old-school Channel U was for me. This book is packed full of amazing superheroes. We have rounded up some of the most talented individuals in their fields — from science to art, and fashion to food — all of whom have turned their special skill, their superpower, into something great.

I also want you to know that we are all superheroes. Each and every one of you has a special skill, a talent, a passion — a superpower — that is unique to you and makes you a superhero.

After reading this book, I hope you know you can achieve whatever you set your mind to. I believe it, and I want you to believe it too. The sky is the limit to what you can achieve, as long as you continue to remember how powerful you are.

AFROCENCHIX

POWER	**TOOL**
Hair	The earth

With every resurrected curl pattern, easy comb-through and breath-taking blow-out, the hair tips of Afrocenchix magicians twist and turn in celebration. Every time a woman grows a new smile at the end of wash-day, Afrocenchix co-founders Rachael and Joycelyn loosen their satin hair-wraps and launch a natural hair festival into the sky. Their tight curls spring towards the sun, absorbing the glorious light that suddenly seems as though it was given as a gift to planet Earth, specifically for black women. The new shine rebounds from head to head, forming a constellation of hair textures and connecting a community of newly natural hair wearers. But with every broken comb, split end, itchy scalp and dry hair, the tips of the Afrocenchix curls shed a tear. Their hair weeps for the 70 per cent of black women who massage harmful chemicals into their gorgeous crowns weekly. The 70 per cent of black women who are still yet to discover Afrocenchix, the hair brand that aims to protect and promote healthy haircare.

The scientists head out into the wild to squeeze nature's elixir into test tubes. They rub palms against leaves and surrender their noses to the intoxicating scents of the world. Once they have unearthed the secrets hidden within the wild, they take their treasure into the lab to create the potions that will remind black hair of its former glory. Ninety-eight per cent of all Afrocenchix products are made from nature's precious alchemy. Mother Nature has always been the best hair stylist for her girls, and the WeWork judges agree. The award-winning brand was the first-ever afro hair brand to launch in Whole Foods.

**Just as our body thrives off the Earth's
natural medicine, so does black hair.**

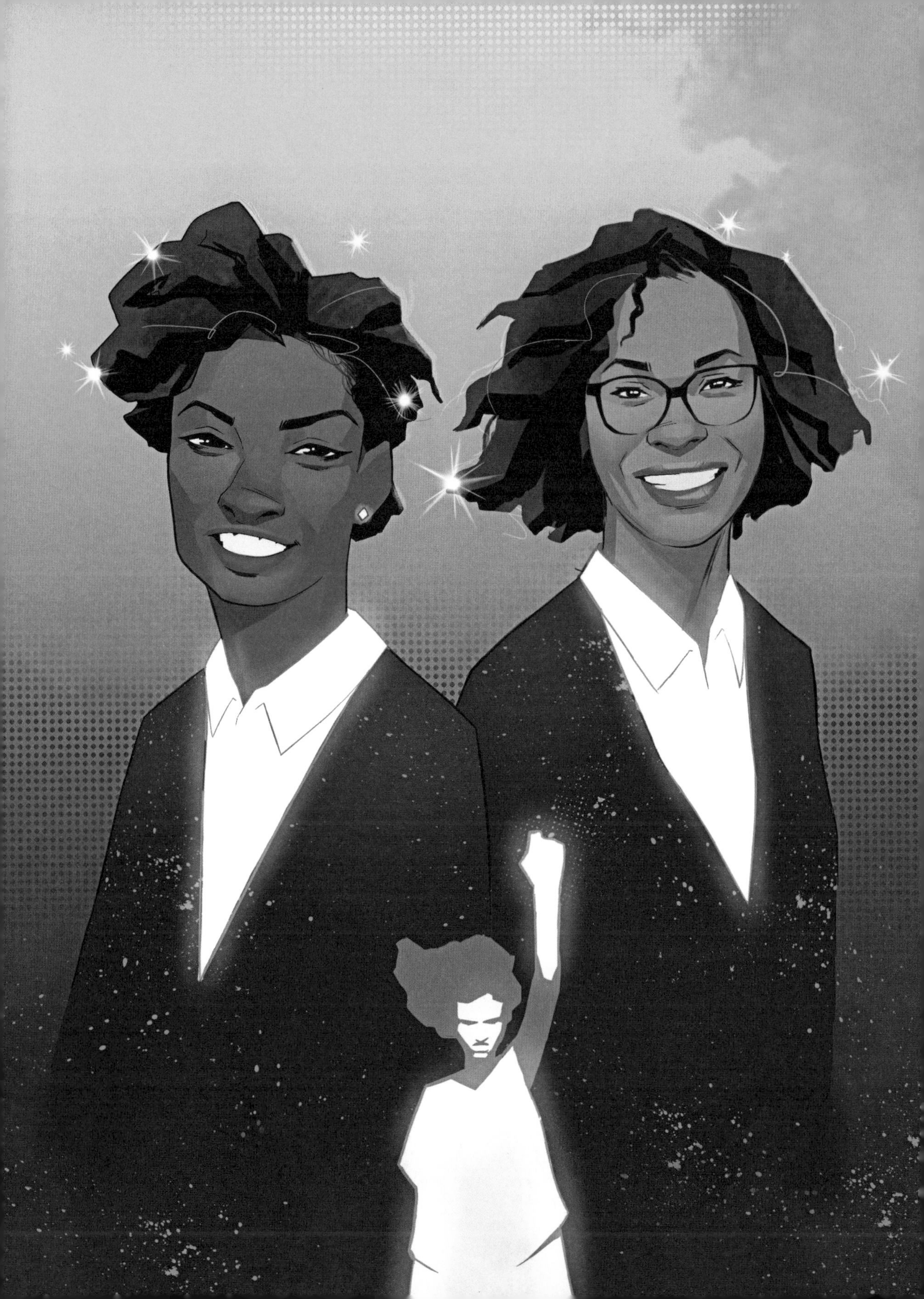

DR ANNE-MARIE IMAFIDON
MBE

POWER
Numbers

TOOL
Brain

Numbers and Anne-Marie Imafidon have always spoken the same language. Whilst the other children would spend weeks learning to count, it came to Anne-Marie in seconds. Her brain could twist a square number into a complex equation and bend itself into an answer with little to no confusion. The only thing confusing for ten-year-old Anne-Marie was why her teachers kept repeating the same things in class. She needed to be challenged, and unfortunately the primary school classrooms just weren't cutting it. At ten years old, she passed two GCSEs in mathematics and ICT. The next year, at eleven years old, she passed two A-level examinations in mathematics and computer science, arguably two of the most difficult subjects for adults — but not for eleven-year-old Anne-Marie. Although the challenge did warm up her brain ever so slightly, it wasn't enough. At seventeen years old she joined a master's degree programme at Oxford University. She graduated at twenty, becoming one of the youngest ever students to graduate with a master's degree.

But Anne-Marie's brain was still only warming up. Along her mind-blowing journey into her brain's full potential, she realised that the opportunities that were given to her weren't available to many young girls. Anne-Marie's desire to share her new industry with other women led her to create Stemettes — a space to tickle the brains of girls and point them towards futures in science, technology, engineering and maths. Through the years, she has found all kinds of young women to mould and nurture into inventors. She speaks children. She speaks numbers. She speaks technology. She speaks Woman of the Year and Powerlists. She also speaks six languages from across the world.

The brain of Anne-Marie Imafidon knows no limits.

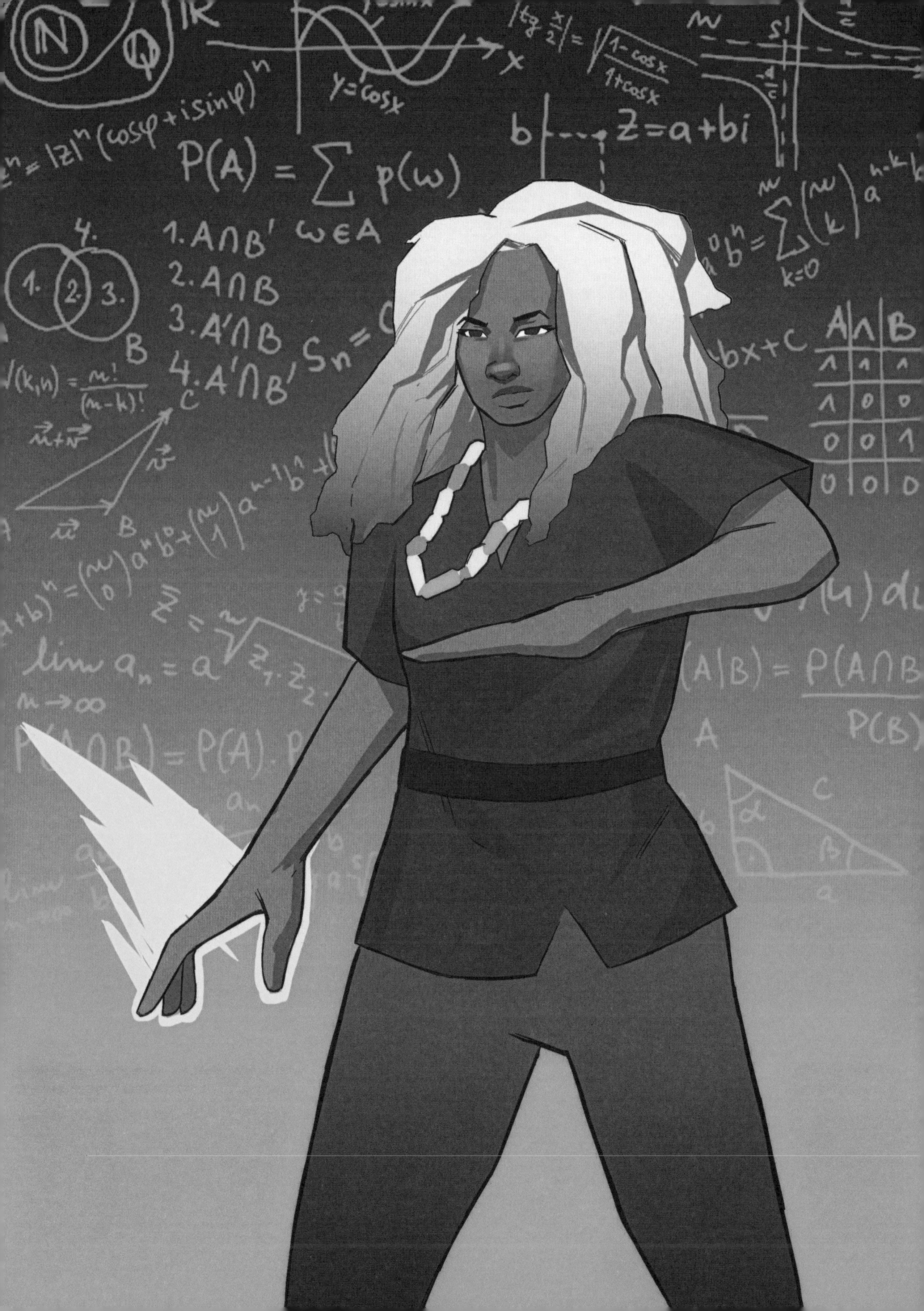

y=cosx
P(A) = ∑ p(ω)
z=a+bi
1. A∩B' ω∈A
2. A∩B
3. A'∩B
4. A'∩B'
lim aₙ = a
n→∞
P(A|B) = P(A∩B) / P(B)

BASMA KHALIFA

POWER
Stylist

TOOL
Images

Let's talk about how things look. About the 100 stories that can be told through an image. An outfit. A news article. A video. A documentary. Sometimes things without mouths speak to us the most. Nobody knows this more than a fashion stylist. Except perhaps a journalist whose task is to pull the stories from the picture. Basma Khalifa is both. She has mastered the silent art of giving mouths to outfits, telling stories of ballroom elegance, urban chic, summer wanderlust and red carpets. But she has also dived head first into images of secretive countries, extracted the story hidden in the shadows of Saudi Arabia. She lived to tell the tale on BBC Three through film and writing, despite the adventure almost costing her her precious life. Basma's skilful and careful capacity to unfold any image to reveal the 100 different things it could be has been refined and shaped across the world. In New York City, she worked in luxury fashion PR, weaving messages into suits and dresses for Mara Hoffman and Jeremy Scott. She did the same again at New York Fashion Week, Miami Fashion Week and London Fashion Week. London is where she really expanded her ability to extract a loud narrative from an image or outfit. Basma Khalifa lends her talent to top brands such as Samsung, Amazon and Kinder, absorbing their commercial briefs and picking the clothes that will tell their story.

What do these trousers say about your company? How do we make her dress tell the story of liberation?

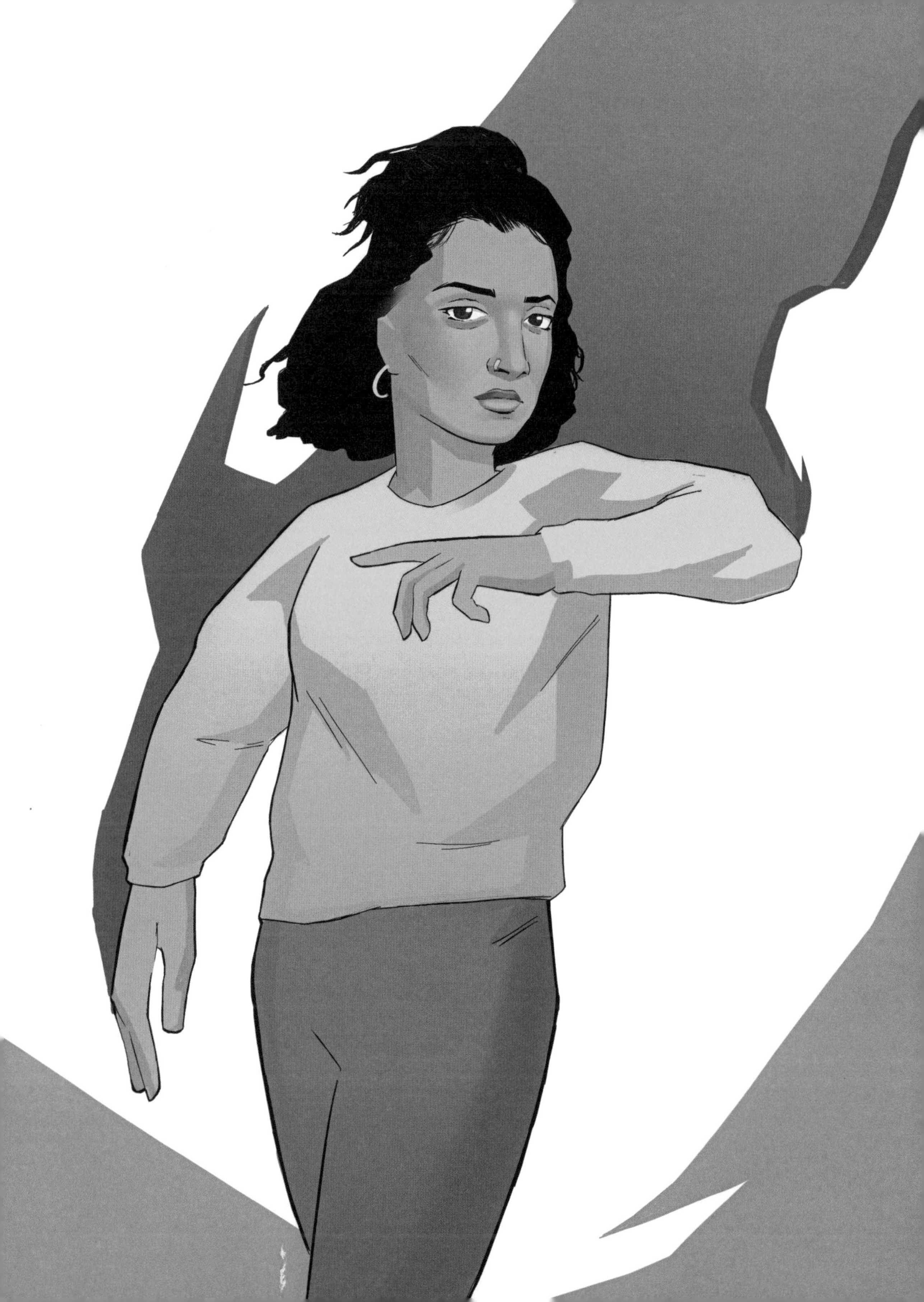

BENJAMINA EBUEHI

POWER	**TOOL**
Flavour	Magic bowl

Caramelised plantain cake. Hot chocolate and halva pudding. White chocolate, lemon and thyme Paris-Brest. Almond cinnamon cake with Irish cream. Hundreds of deliciously designed recipes and treats race around the magic mixing bowl. A playground of edible excellence that starts in the scrumptious brain of Benjamina Ebuehi. Since the age of fourteen, Benjamina has enjoyed a very personal relationship with mixing bowls. In the curve of her palms, her wildest creations come alive, tantalising both taste buds and eyes. The magic that is made in those bowls is so strong and so tasty that even through a television, her delicious cakes and bakes cause viewers across the country to salivate and slide their way into their own kitchens to try to recreate the magic in their own mixing bowls.

To satisfy the country's hunger for such sweet treats, Benjamina released a cookery book *The New Way to Cake* (and has a new one in the pipeline: *A Good Day to Bake*, for Spring 2022). Within these pretty, pretty pages, Benjamina's Nigerian heritage, British upbringing and masterful eye for food styling come together to revolutionise classic recipes that are sure to stretch a smile across any stomach.

Benjamina competed in *The Great British Bake Off*, wowing the nation with how easily she made a plate look like a perfect painting of foods. With a keen eye for beauty, the brand Glossier called on Benjamina to host one of her infamous Sister Table brunches: a finger-licking movement she started with her sisters to bring women together to break bread and slice cakes. The magic that lives in her mixing bowl is craved everywhere. From Amazon to her column in the *Guardian*, Benjamina Ebuehi awakens the stomachs of people everywhere.

When in doubt... choose cake.

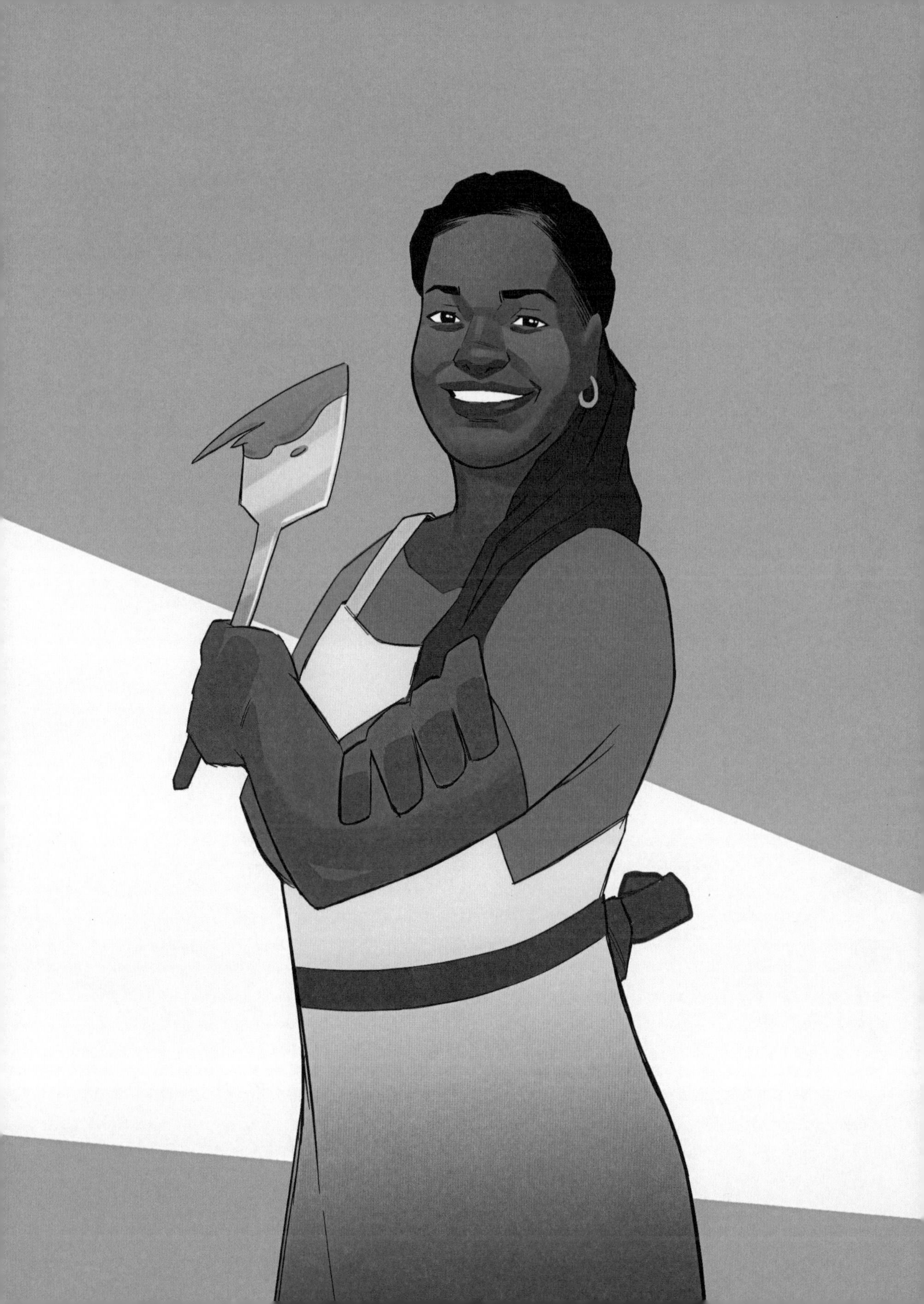

BIANCA SAUNDERS

POWER
Menswear

TOOL
Sewing machine

They twisted to the rhythm of dancehall, gathered and stretched, floated and skimmed the skin of Bianca's uncles as the Caribbean men surrendered their bodies to the sound. Their clothes danced with them, mirroring their movement, the smiles, the moves that did not need to be in Jamaica to feel right at home. In this South London party, the outfits were given the chance to remember how it felt to be enjoyed.

As a young girl, Bianca Saunders sat with her cousins, soaking in how the clothes and the men danced together. The draped shirts and flowy trousers became her first memory of menswear that encouraged expression and comfort. The memories danced around her mind to the sound of home, and at fourteen years old, after being encouraged by her parents to pursue whichever career she wanted, Bianca made the decision to explore what could be created behind a sewing machine. She was going to design a menswear line that oozed freedom of expression and movement.

Whilst studying fashion at the elite Royal College of Art, her blackness became one of the loudest things about her. After all, she was the only black student. Without the option to forget that she came from a different world to the other students, she pulled those memories into the realm of high fashion. Years on we have the musical composition of her clothing line: Bianca Saunders.

Bianca dresses the men who make us move, from Wizkid to Jvck James. Her collections have walked and danced their way down many Fashion Week runways and into almost all of the top magazines, from *Vanity Fair* to *Vogue*.

The feelings in her clothes are craved by the fashion world as much as freedom is craved by us all.

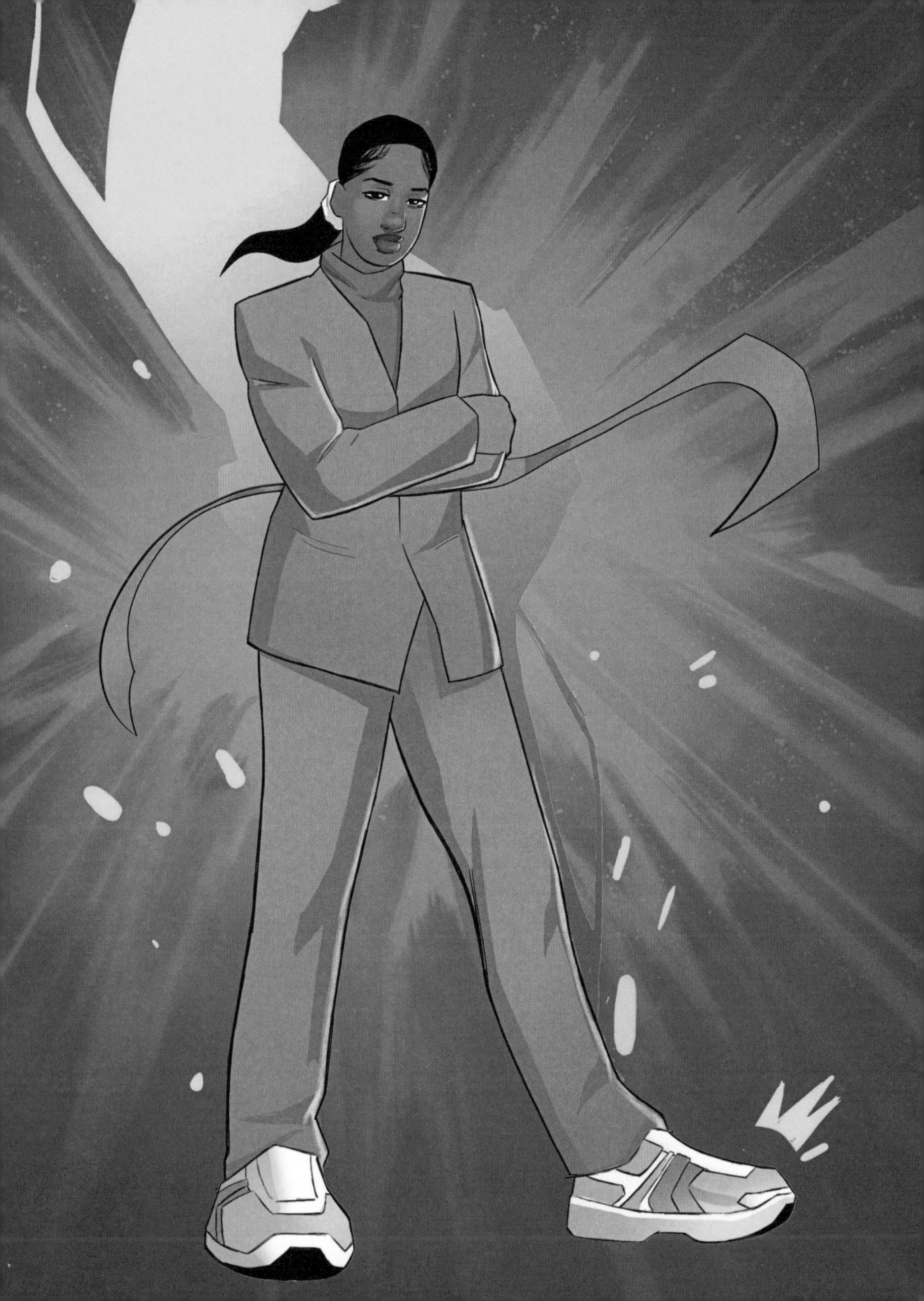

BOLA AGBAJE

POWER
Playwriting

TOOL
Magical mind

Like flowers blooming from concrete in double time, lives and characters burst up through the page and onto the stage, becoming everything that Bola Agbaje had imagined in her magical mind. It was 2006, and the stories that had played out around Bola and the estate she grew up in had had time to settle into the belly of her brain.

Bola Agbaje knows diaspora tensions well. She knows estate loyalty and how it can cost lives. She knows how confusing the idea of 'home' can become whilst living in the UK. She sees it in the faces of her friends as they wait and wonder when they will see their experiences reflected on stage and TV. These stories have lived inside Bola, waiting for their grand opening. And finally, after the Royal Court Theatre's Young Writers Programme nurtured her writing voice, Bola's first play was given the space to bloom into more than memories and imagination. *Gone Too Far!* emerged straight from the magical mind of Bola and captured the essence of cultural clashes so well that it did more than just entertain audiences — it made minority groups that often get overlooked or are misrepresented in the arts, feel seen. Valued.

The integrity of the play earned her a prestigious Laurence Olivier Award for her outstanding achievement. *Gone Too Far!* was requested and revived for second and third theatre runs at the iconic Hackney Empire and the Albany Theatre. Bola Agbaje has since gone on to bring her stories to the big screen!

It's all cyclical — the living happens, and then it gets given a stage, and then, with what we learn from plays like *Belong*, we try to fix our reality.

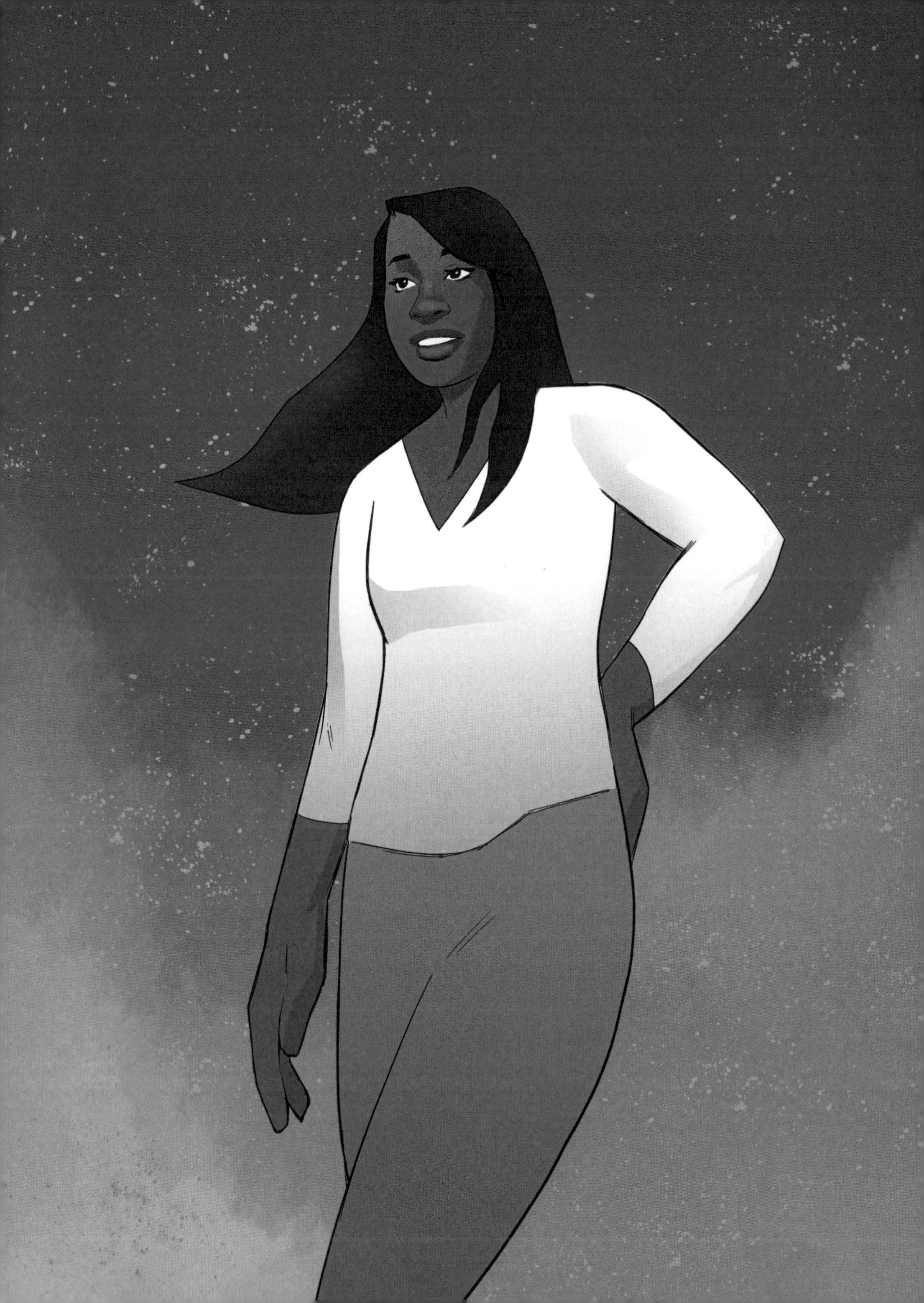

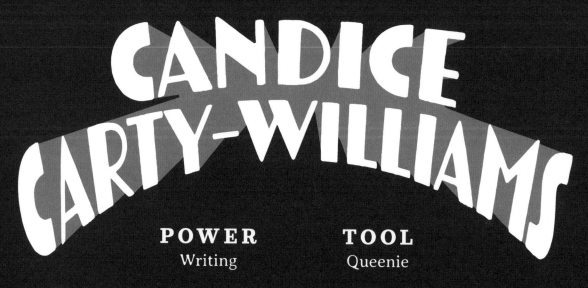

CANDICE CARTY-WILLIAMS

POWER
Writing

TOOL
Queenie

There always seemed to be something trying to silence her. Candice Carty-Williams spent her early years being pushed further and further away from her self-confidence, in the way that only school and those traumatising teen years can do. One day, after being excluded from school for a week, she discovered a safe space where people would not judge her, or compare her, or touch her hair. Between the arms of Lewisham Library, where she'd been banished for the week, Candice made reading her refuge. Suddenly her days became pages and her years became chapters. Her 'book of the year', *Queenie*, began writing itself on the inside of her eyes, without Candice even knowing. Like the North Star, *Queenie* was secretly guiding Candice into her destiny as an author.

That Candice later found herself working in marketing for the publishing houses 4th Estate and Vintage was no coincidence. But during her time there, the racism and lack of representation in the publishing industry was fully revealed to her. So, together with 4th Estate and the *Guardian*, Candice created an opportunity for under-represented writers to find their place on the shelves. And finally, after watching so many young black voices step into their confidence, Candice was ready for *Queenie* to come alive. On the first night of a writing retreat at Jojo Moyes' house, 8,000 words flooded onto the page, to be joined by another 40,000 after just a week — *Queenie* was ready to meet all of the bestseller lists and literary prizes as a young, black, realistic twenty-first-century adult.

Queenie is the story of getting it wrong but feeling all right enough to try again with love and life.

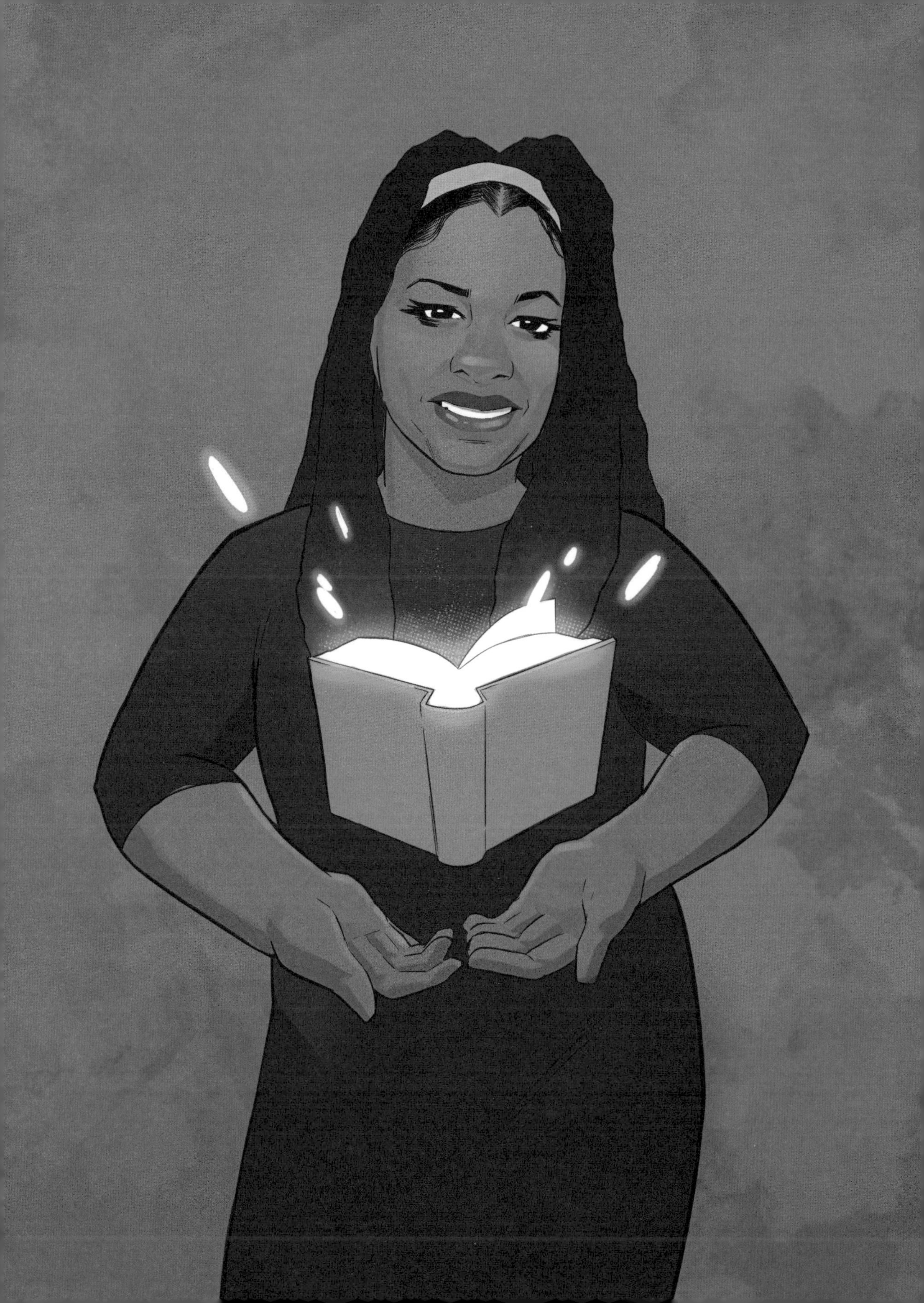

CECE PHILIPS

POWER
Art

TOOL
Paintbrush

Toni Morrison once said that art has the responsibility of introducing moral imagination to the audience. It reserves this rare right to reimagine life in a way that makes us want to do it differently. To see people differently. To think more widely about a person, place or culture. Cece Philips' paintings demand the opening of the human eye and mind, the reimagination of black life in colour. To lift the idea of 'blackness' off the history textbook and news headline, and gently layer our lenses with a sheet of possibility. Her artwork runs soft, oil-dipped paintbrushes over our eyes and asks us to remember that black people are vibrant. They are soft pink suits and sultry oranges walking to work with friends. They are jazz-coloured afternoons catching up with the brothers, and they are electric, deep reds, the colour of lineage.

Cece Philips has always loved painting real life. On Friday evenings, she would find herself sat in front of humans, painting them in the shades of their essence. Her love for reimagining took her to Florence to study how others have done it before her, and in a year that brought a grey cloud over the entire world, Cece Philips committed all of her time to putting colour back into people's days. Her first art exhibition, *I See In Colour*, reminds us that we can live as loudly as we desire.

Our narrative is ours to reclaim.

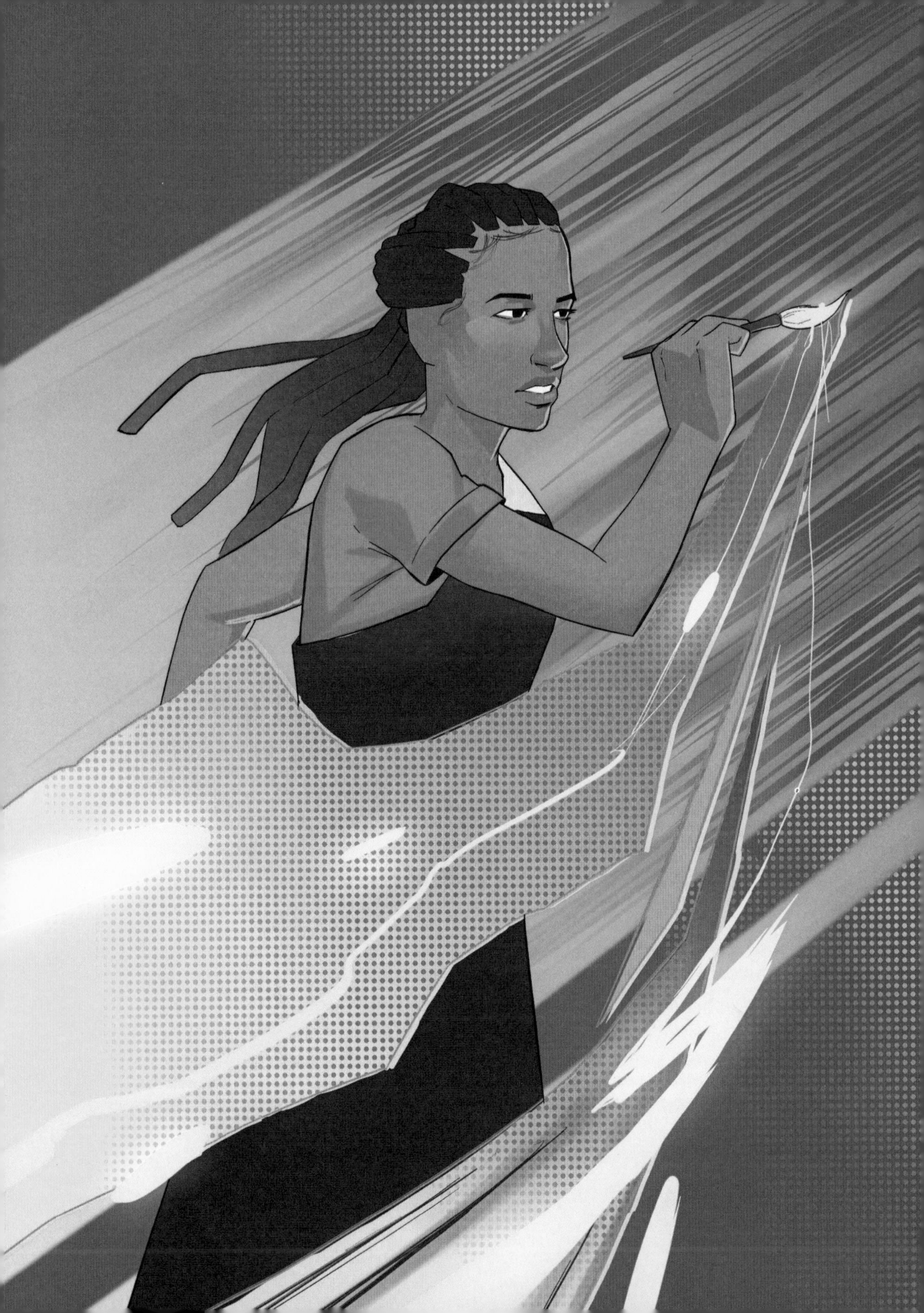

CHARLENE WHITE

POWER
Presenting

TOOL
Tunnel of truth

Tucked into the front right corner of her mind sits a converter. Some call it a translator, others a tunnel of truth. It is more commonly known as a presenter's thought process, but that would not do Charlene White's tool justice. She does not just present information back to us. She pulls stories from their place of birth into the delicate, intricate machine of her mind. There they are pumped full of power, honesty, vulnerability and inspiration. It is no wonder that almost every station has sought this remarkable mind's machine. From starting out as a presenter of a two-hour documentary programme for BBC 1Xtra, she moved on to ITV to become the first black woman to present the *ITV News at Ten*. And it is no surprise that she has found herself on the Powerlist as one of the top 100 most influential people of African and Caribbean heritage in the United Kingdom. The machine of her mind not only pulls the gold from stories, but also the truth, to be fed back to the people in such a way that it is understood by all ages. As a black Caribbean woman, her mind's machine has had to understand and forgive racism time and time again to be able to explain movements such as Black Lives Matter to people with the help of other super-minds like Sir Trevor McDonald, and for younger viewers on the TV show, *IRL with Team Charlene*.

Charlene White's groundbreaking mind has made the world a little bit smaller and more connected, by presenting stories in a way that only she can.

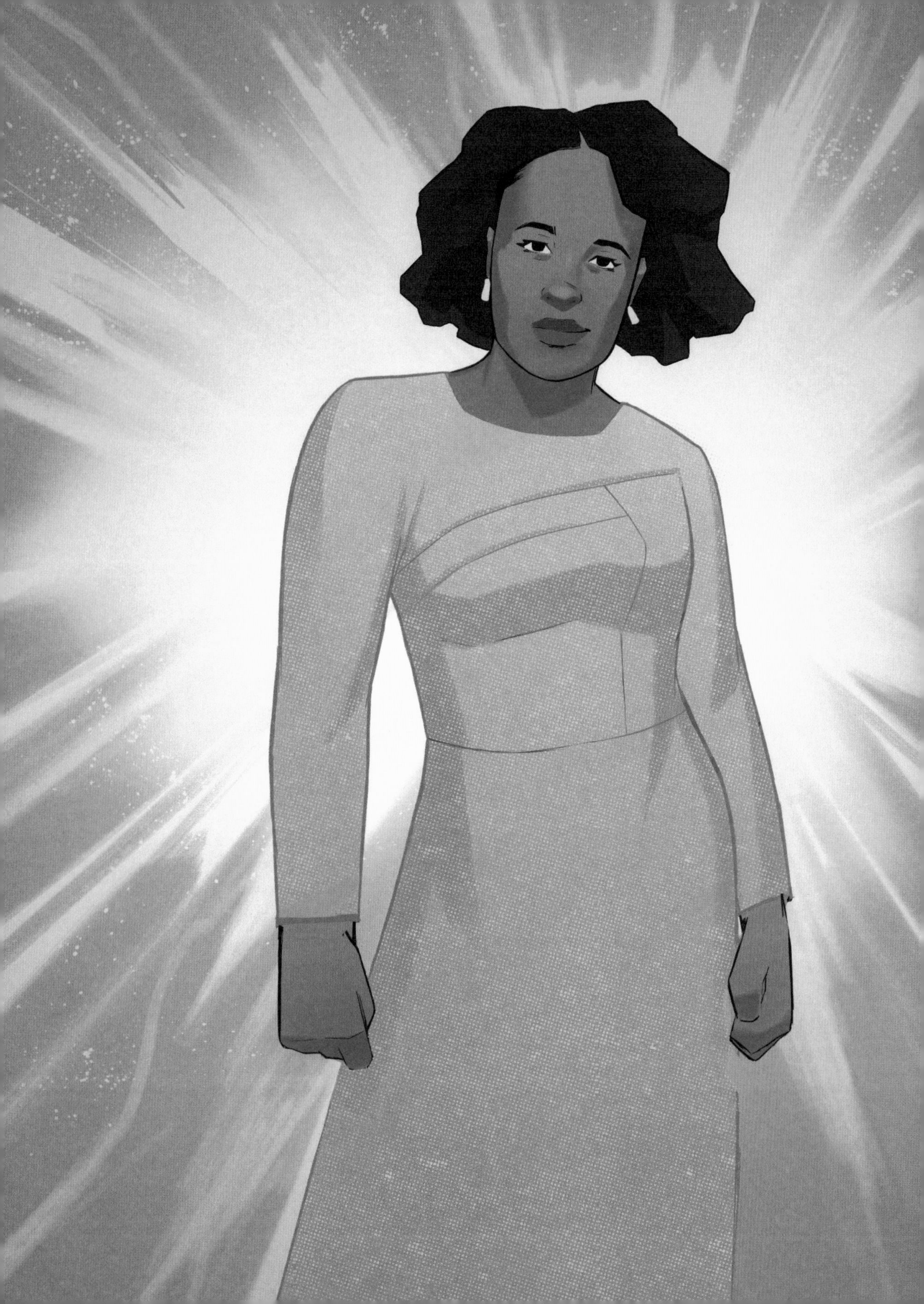

CHARLIE CASELY-HAYFORD

POWER
Suits

TOOL
Fashion

Most kids' growth is tracked on a door frame in the family home. Charlie Casely-Hayford's height was tracked by suit trousers and jacket seams from his parents' design studio. At eighteen months, Charlie's first cape was designed in the form of a three-piece suit. As collars were straightened and ties were pulled tight, the outfit became more than just the envy of every parent at each function. It became the uniform that would travel forward to find Charlie years later whilst he was studying. His time at university was spent exploring the history of art, and there he met his future. Charlie became fascinated with fashion's silent but roaring ability to speak on the times. Every trouser cut had a story behind it. Each neckline adorned the chest of a decade that could be remembered by its stitching alone. Charlie's eye grew notably delicate and specific, and the world became obsessed with his runway. He was named one of *GQ*'s '50 best-dressed men in Britain'. But his new connection with fashion went beyond him. He joined his father in setting up the award-winning luxury menswear label Casely-Hayford. Since then, he has clothed many industries in his expertise. He has dressed the stars, from Drake to Sam Smith. He has styled the magazines, from *GQ* to *i-D*. As the years fill his suit, the wisdom that he soaked in from his parents as a boy spills out both in the design studio and on camera. Charlie's expertise had him named one of the 100 most important people in fashion. Converse and Dr. Martens, two retail giants that believe in fashion's relationship with history, fell in love with the man in the perfectly tailored suit, and had to make him the face of their campaigns.

For Charlie Casely-Hayford, it's more than fashion. It is family.

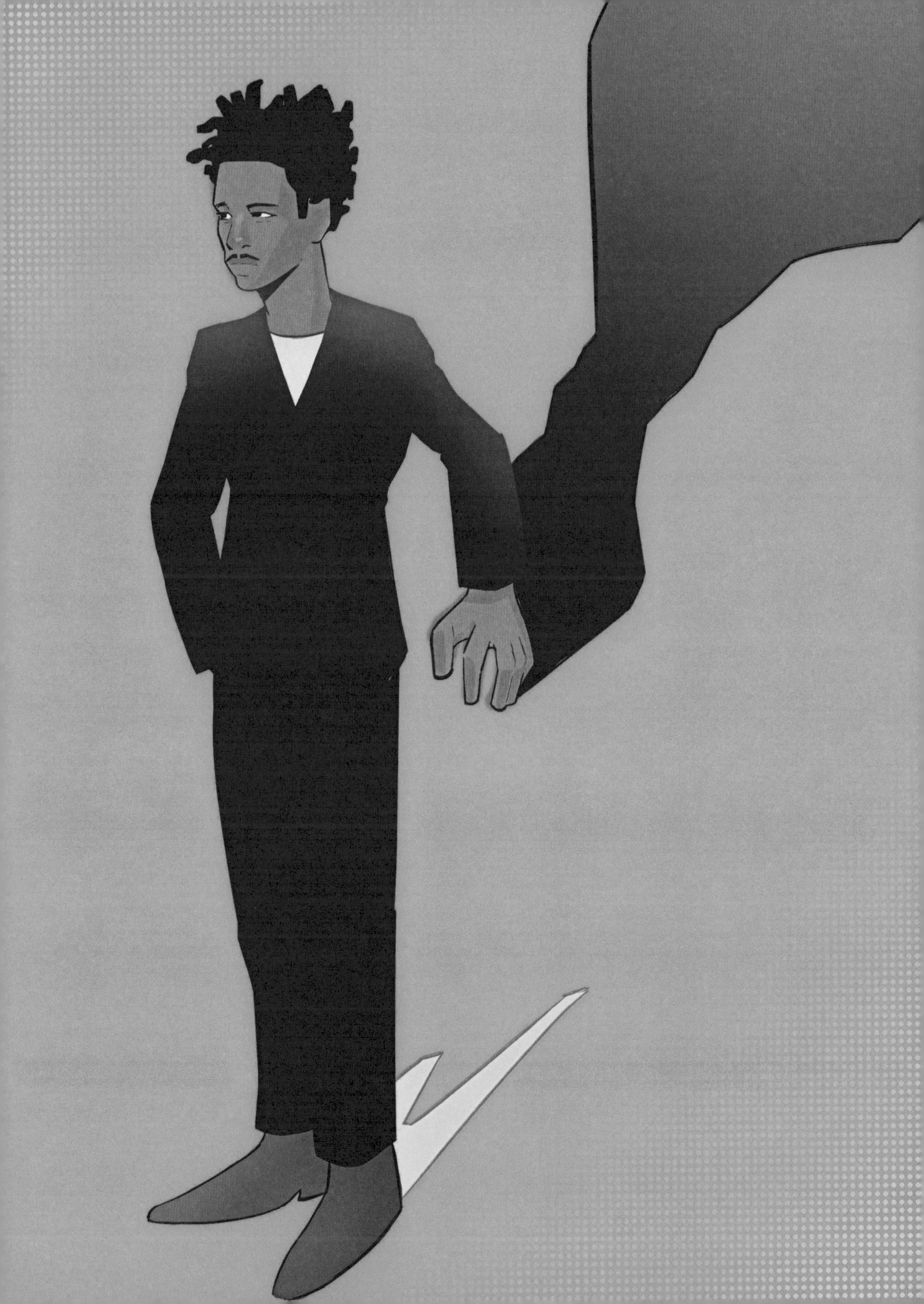

CHI-CHI NWANOKU

OBE

POWER
Music

TOOL
Her heart

Everything is musical. The pitch of the wind during a storm. The rhythm of raindrops against our window. The hum of birds and the melody of laughter. The earth is wrapped in one ever-changing song, and our hearts dance with its pulse. Some of us enjoy it quietly, but for a chosen few that choice was never their own. Chi-chi Nwanoku was powerless against the tug music had on her heart. At the age of seven, her pulse would stop for the first time whilst playing the piano. A rare phenomenon occurred under her skin: her heart became still and her body was powered by the sounds of music alone. From that day, she knew that music was to be a huge part of her survival. And since then, her heart has resided in various instruments, eventually finding a home in the double bass.

Chi-chi Nwanoku's intimate kinship with music is a marvel to witness and hear. Her thrilling recordings include Schubert's Trout Quintet and his Octet, Beethoven's Septet, Boccherini's sonatas, Vanhal's and Dittersdorf's concertos. To anyone who's had the pleasure of hearing her play, it's no surprise that she was in the top ten of the BBC Women in Music Power List 2018.

Chi-chi works hard to ensure that black people are given a chance to give their hearts some songs in an unfair world through her foundation, Chineke! Her intimate dedication to sound and song goes beyond just the playing, but lies deep in the history of double bass.

Her heart becomes instrumental in teaching the timeless power of music to the people.

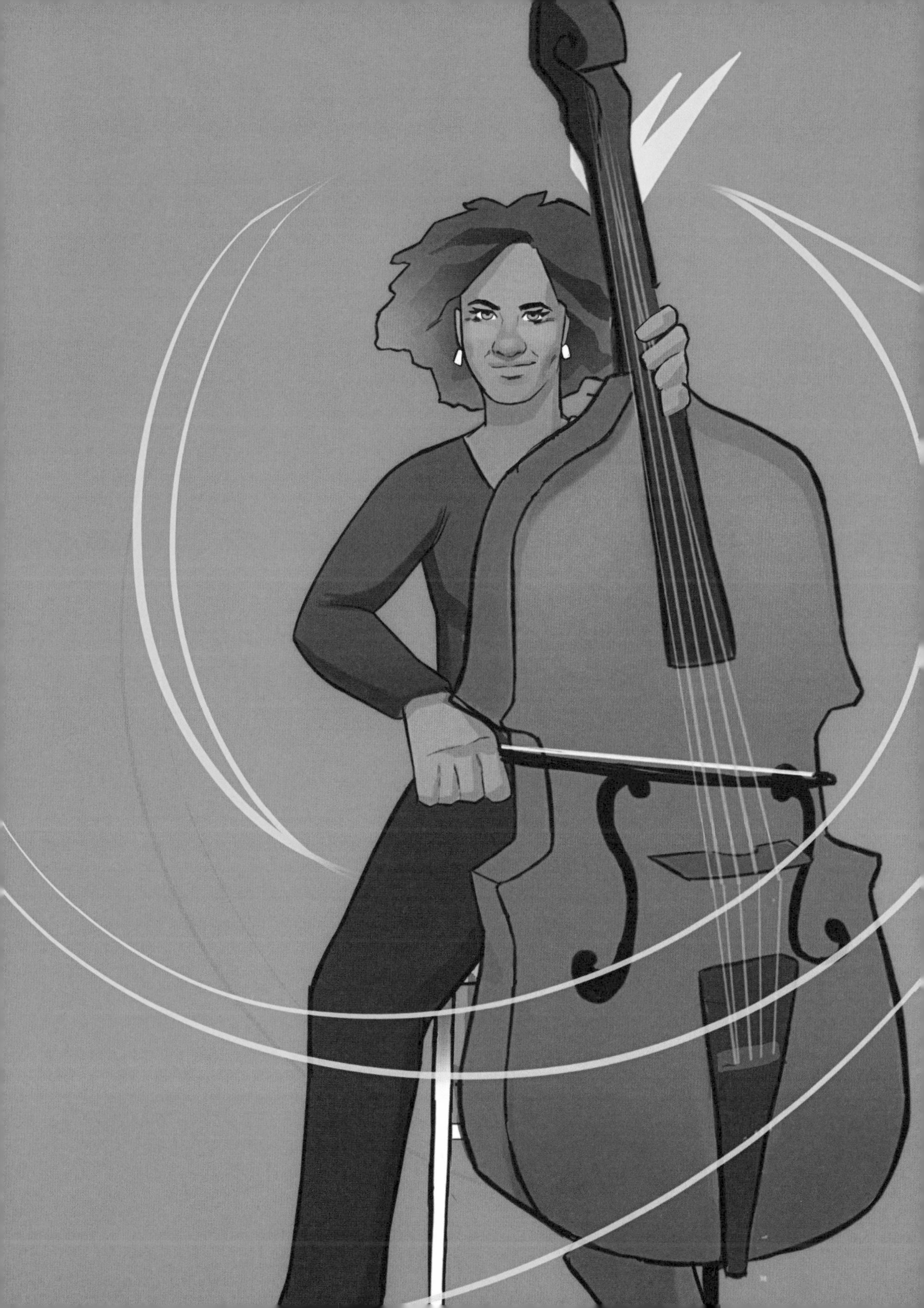

DR CLIFFORD V. JOHNSON

POWER
Physics

TOOL
Tunnel of communication

They all put their trust in him. The current that runs through the air. The plug sockets in your homes. The aeroplanes you climb into. The sky above you and all of the earth. We rest as easily as we do because scientists like Clifford V. Johnson exist to keep everything that is unseen by the standard human eye, balanced and in order. This allows us to go about our normal lives without the worry of science ever turning against us. He is the guardian of our galaxy, checking in daily with gravity, black holes and the particles around us. Whilst books and essays wait to be written by him, we wait to be taught how the elements around us behave and what they need from us to help them continue to serve all of the earth.

In 2005, Clifford won the James Clerk Maxwell Medal for his outstanding contributions to the understanding of quantum gravity. He remains one of the most-cited black professors in American universities and colleges, and the National Science Foundation awarded him the Career Award for his brilliance in interpreting the world around him. His award-winning explanations of the sacred connection between science and humans has kept us safe.

To some, he may just seem like a genius scientist with a graphic science book and lots of university students. But, to those who share a similar power, he is recognised as one of the finest super scientists of our time. Even The Avengers called on him to ensure that the quantum world around them was kept in order, so that they could go on to save the earth in movies. The *National Geographic* reaches out to him to share any new messages from Planet Earth. Clifford recognised how unique his abilities are, but also how important it was to share them. So he put on a month-long conference: the African Summer Theory Institute. Here, he gathered teachers, researchers and students to share some of the secrets to the universe.

Slowly, Clifford V. Johnson awakens his own genius group of Avengers to explain the world.

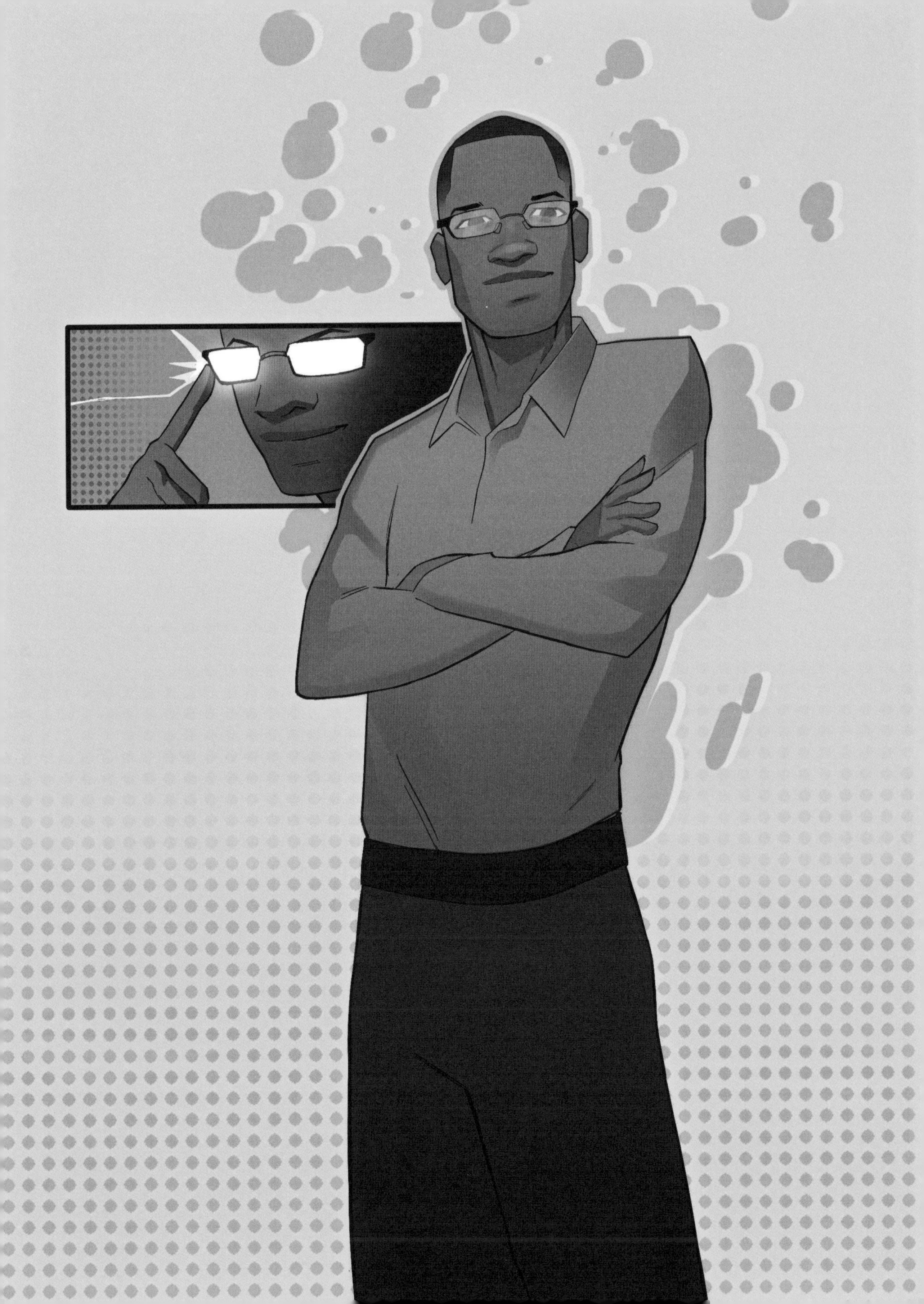

COMUZI

POWER
Seeing the future

TOOL
Technology

The ideas were there, brewing inside the minds of Alex Fefegha and Akil Benjamin. New technology flashed in their eyes, something very special happened when they blinked: a vision of how organisations could co-design more equitable futures with communities was born.

Alex and Akil knew exactly what they needed to do. Kind of. There weren't many people that looked like them in the industry. Black, that is. So, whilst running Comuzi, the company for the future they envisioned, they put on suits and bow ties to try and look more like the creative technology company owners they had seen. But as time passed, they realised that their differences were actually a strength, not a weakness. ASOS, Nike, the BBC and Citizens Advice needed their expertise because who else would help organisations become future-fit with minority groups in mind?

The suits came off, and the dreadlocks were unleashed. Company-by-company, panel-by-panel, Alex and Akil slowly released their visions of the future into as many new spaces as possible, whilst also ensuring that young black creatives wanting to work in the tech industry did not face the same challenges that they did. Akil set up Mentor Black Business, a programme that trains black creatives and entrepreneurs to unlock their own superpowers, and even gives them the tools to do it. Emerging from backgrounds where careers in design and advertising were not encouraged, the boys experienced the mental battle of working against the grain. This led Alex to also set up Safe Space — a place to take off their super suits, put their phones away and just be really honest about how difficult it can be to be a superhero sometimes.

In releasing what is so heavy, the world can see how high they can fly once they let go.

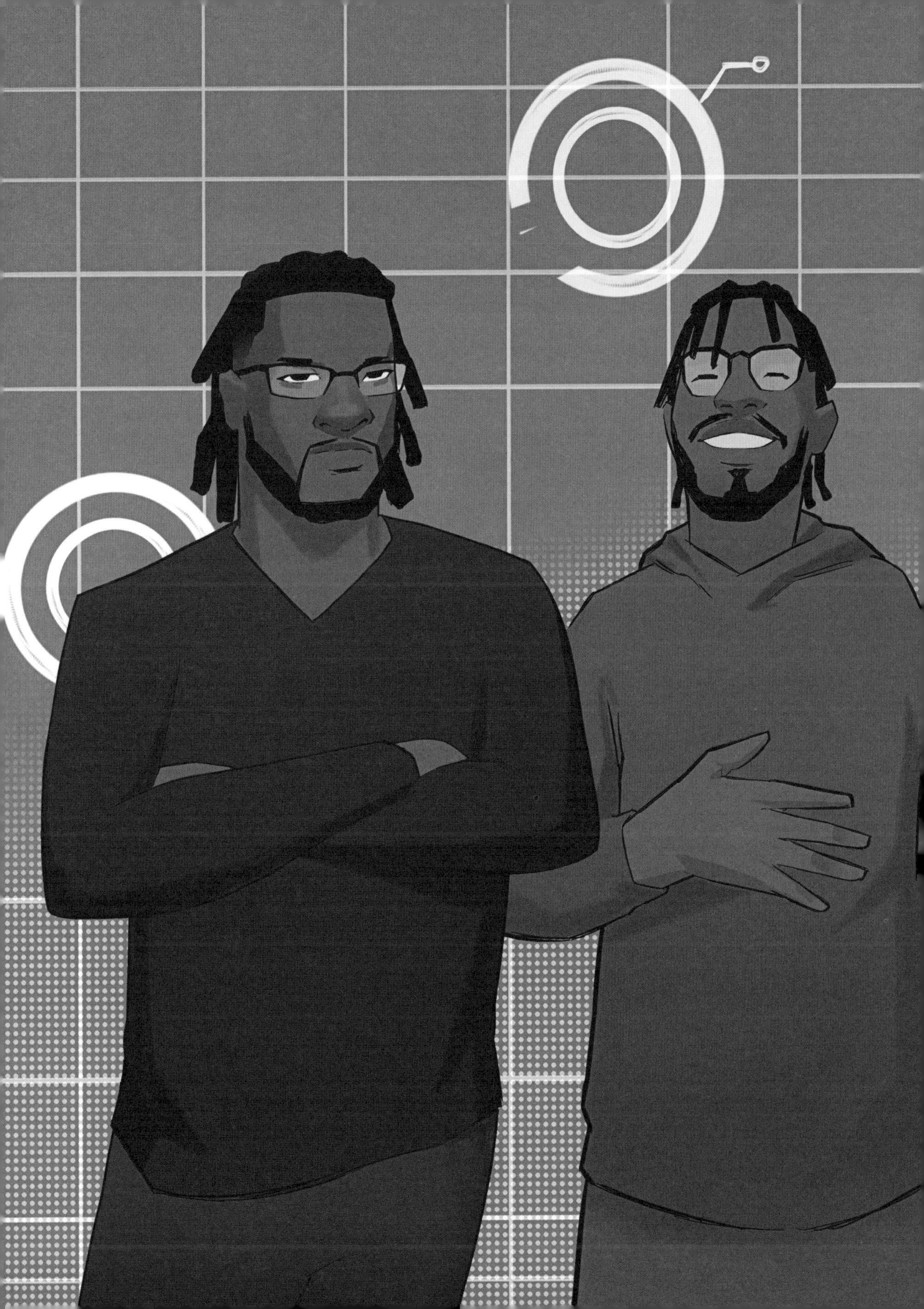

CRAIG & SHAUN McANUFF

POWER
Reinventing food

TOOL
Noses

They rise in spiralling spells, charming the nostrils of the hungry. The scent of home, of white sandy beaches and fresh fruit, breaks through borders and pins people to the Caribbean islands. But for two brothers, Craig and Shaun McAnuff, the sweet aromas of frying Scotch bonnets and stewing chicken did not just travel into their noses with memories of Jamaica. The smells went all the way up and around their brains, triggering new visions of what Caribbean food could become.

As the smells swim past the brothers' eyes, they see flashbacks from the stories their grandmother would tell them about how food was the thing that brought Caribbean people together in England when they arrived as the 'Windrush generation', at a time when many Caribbeans felt so far from home.

The smells continue shooting around Shaun and Craig, creating colourful and flavour-filled recipe ideas from their imaginations: plantain burgers, shrimp mac and cheese. With no other option but to give these visions a place to land, the boys created the bestselling cookbook *Original Flava: Caribbean Recipes from Home*, a mix of their grandmother's stories and dishes, their vibrant remixes of traditional recipes, stories from locals and even a vegan chapter. In 2019, as the book flew off the shelves, carrying that same delicious power with it, people everywhere fell under the spell of *Original Flava*, and they needed more. Whilst balancing *GQ*, Asda and Sainsbury's campaigns (where they used to work), the brothers also started an online Caribbean food festival of virtual cooking classes in partnership with Jamie Oliver and created a food calendar for people to track their days via their taste buds.

On building a road to delicious food, they have led the people into the heart of the island.

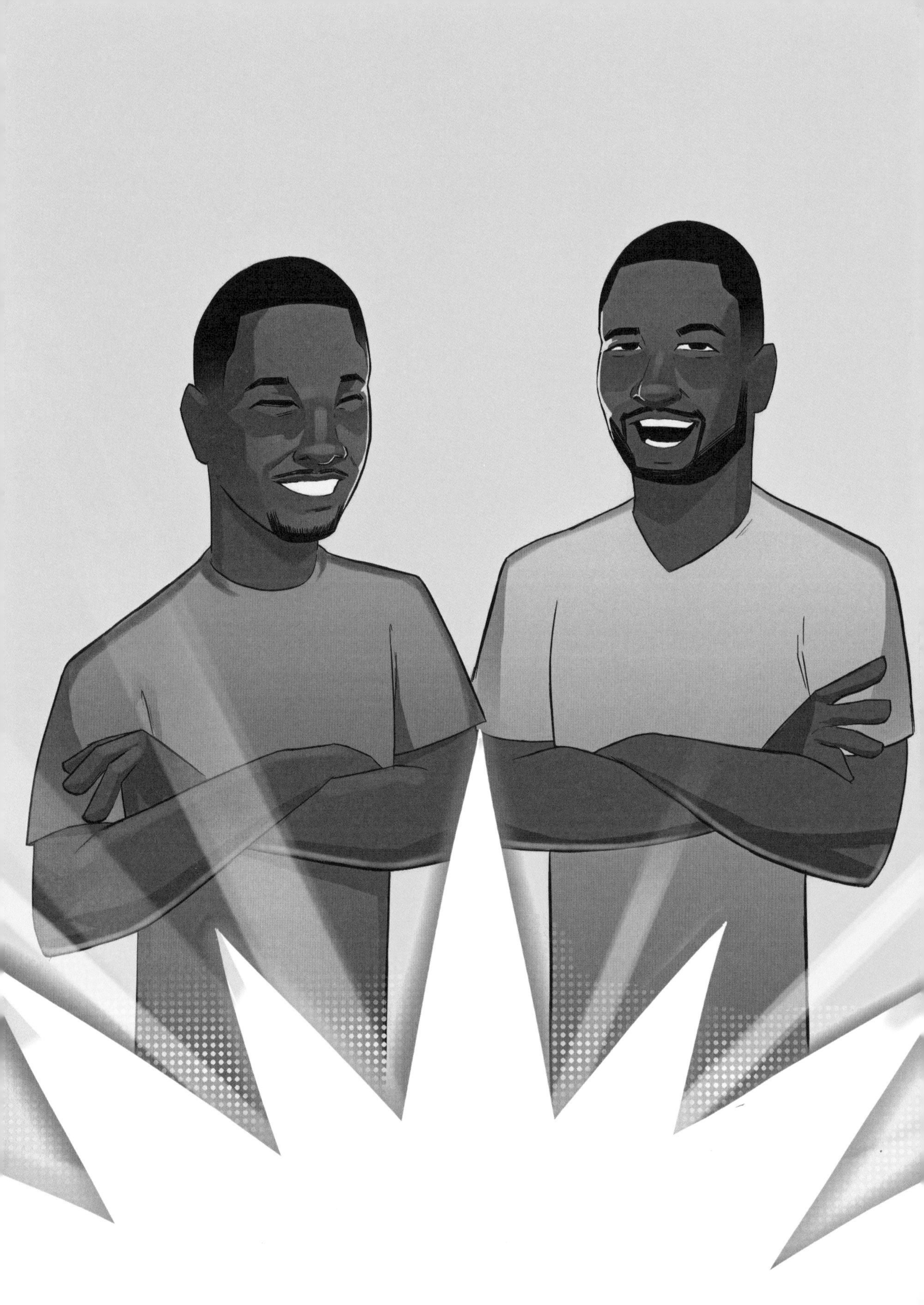

DINA ASHER-SMITH

POWER
Speed

TOOL
Running spikes

Thousands of young girls watched as Kelly Holmes was crowned on the podium in Athens in 2004. But something in the stars shifted as a girl in Orpington watched and decided at the age of eight that she too would be crowned one day. Dina Asher-Smith's lightning speed had been waiting for this moment to come so that it could explode within her.

As Dina first slides her feet into the lips of her running spikes, sparks erupt, electrifying her legs and activating a speed even faster than her teacher. As she journeys through school and university, she becomes faster and faster with each race, pushing towards better results on and off the athletics track. Her school grades have always taken first place, sitting as invisible medals around her already very crowded neck. I guess when you're running at top speeds, the only safe option is to win. At everything.

The year is 2019. As 23-year-old super-speed Dina takes to her knee on the blocks at the World Athletics Championships, the nation holds its breath to witness this power in action. Unlike most superheroes, Dina's power at the starting line is activated by fear. It rumbles in her belly and pours into her legs. But, once it touches the rim of her spikes, that fear explodes, like fireworks within her, stunning the whole stadium with her breath-stealing power. The crowd erupts in cheers as she shoots from the starting line to make history as the fastest woman in Britain.

**Failure falls on its face when faced with
Dina Asher-Smith's super-speed.**

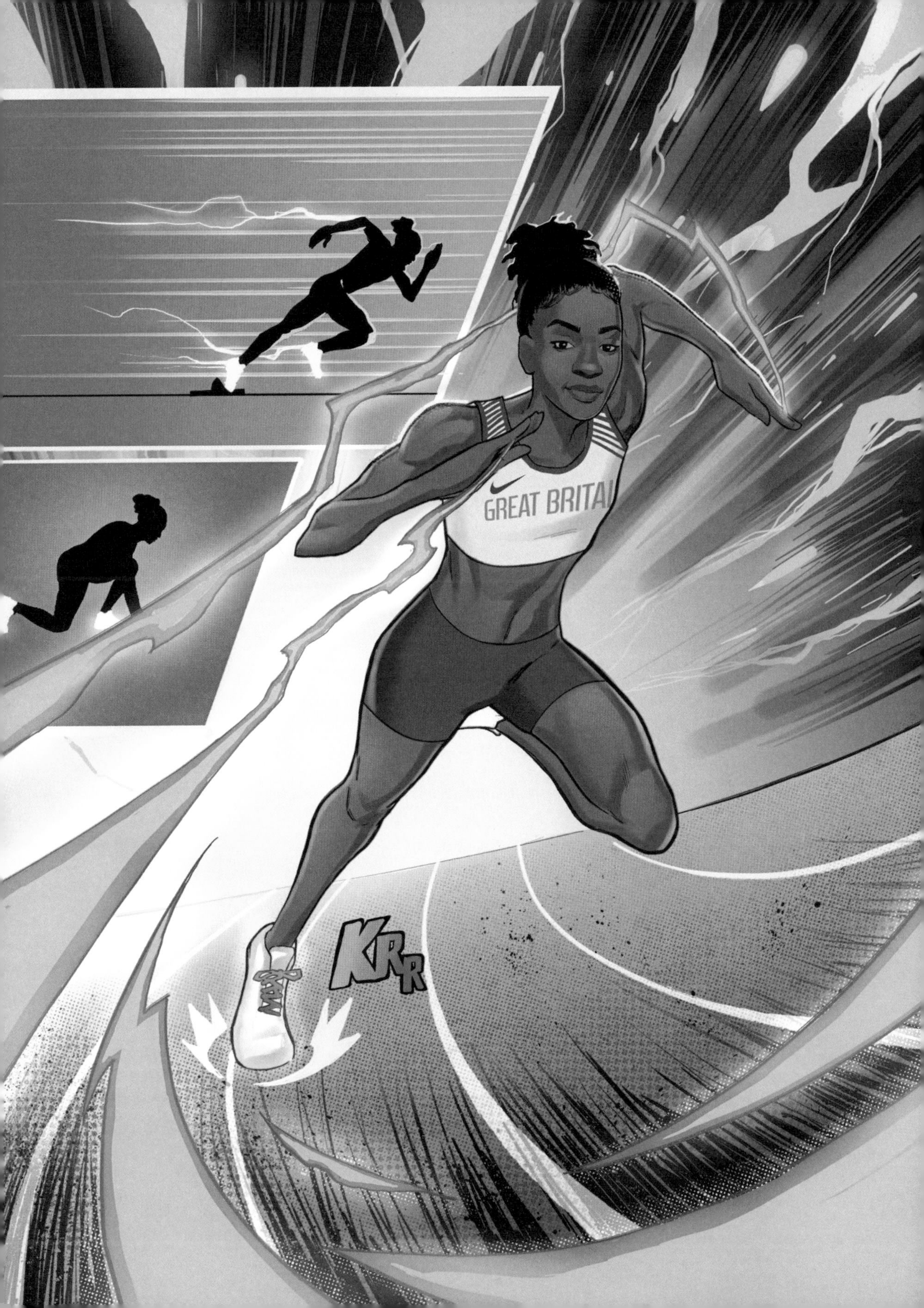
GREAT BRITAI
KRRR

DOWNIE SISTERS

POWER
Gymnastics

TOOL
Kaleidoscope eyes

Kaleidoscope eyes rotate in the faces of Becky and Ellie Downie. Life is presented to them in spinning, sequined seasons and upside-down days. Whilst most people look at a thin balance bench as something to approach with caution, the sisters' kaleidoscope eyes see a platform to flip around or balance on.

Life never stopped being a playground to Becky and Ellie, the two sisters who activate their powers to contort their bodies into increasingly complex shapes and poses. As they blink into their kaleidoscope vision, their bodies obey immediately and launch both sisters into a fairground of artistic, gymnastic fun.

Becky Downie gathered the air from everyone's lungs at the 2008 and 2016 Olympic Games, entire stadiums freezing as she whizzed through the air like a bird. She lands as delicately as a feather onto podiums at the European Championships, World Championships and the Commonwealth Games. And the entire world held its breath at the 2017 European Artistic Gymnastics Championships, as Ellie Downie turned the gymnasium floor into a playground in her head, flipping her way to a gold medal — making her the first British athlete to win this event.

Everything is better in twos
— especially the Downies.

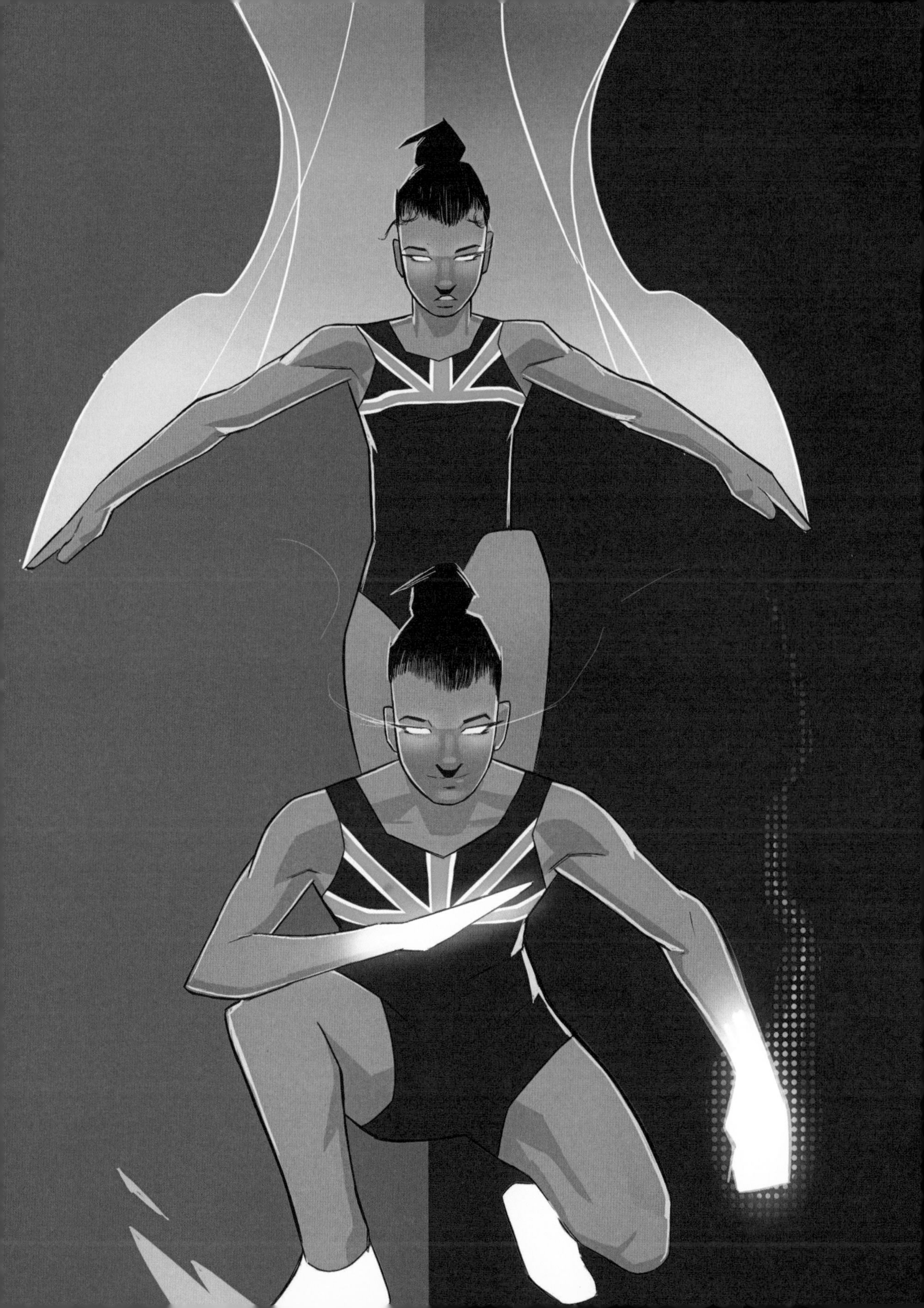

EMMANUELLE LHONI

POWER
Communicating with
the weather

TOOL
The elements

With a spoonful of sun and a cup of clouds racing around Emmanuelle's glowing body, it was only a matter of time before her top-secret relationship with the weather would be revealed on the world stage. But first, she had to appease her parents and fulfil her duty to her education. The only problem was — there simply wasn't time! The sky needed her to communicate what was going to happen above human heads — immediately. So, with all of the heavens on her side, a shooting star was triggered within her and launched her into important rooms. The sky knew that, in order for Emmanuelle to be able to share what the sky needed people to know, she would have to do what had not yet been done in her immediate family: get a degree. A super-suit that the world recognised.

A message was sent down with the rain and soon the Russell Group universities caught wind of Emmanuelle's unique affinity with the atmosphere. She was delivered to the doors of the University of Leeds — the only Russell Group university at the time to have a broadcast journalism course. This course would equip her with the tools she needed to wield to read the sky. One of the most important weapons that she picked up whilst studying was passion. It drove her to collect her master's degree in international journalism, igniting her bilingual powers and enabling her to tell the stories of English and French-speaking countries for the BBC World Service. Emmanuelle was hired as the first Congolese and, currently, the youngest black female weather presenter at the BBC. The sun inside her now beams out its plans on our television screens.

The entire sky exhales into the safe and skilled hands of Emmanuelle Lhoni.

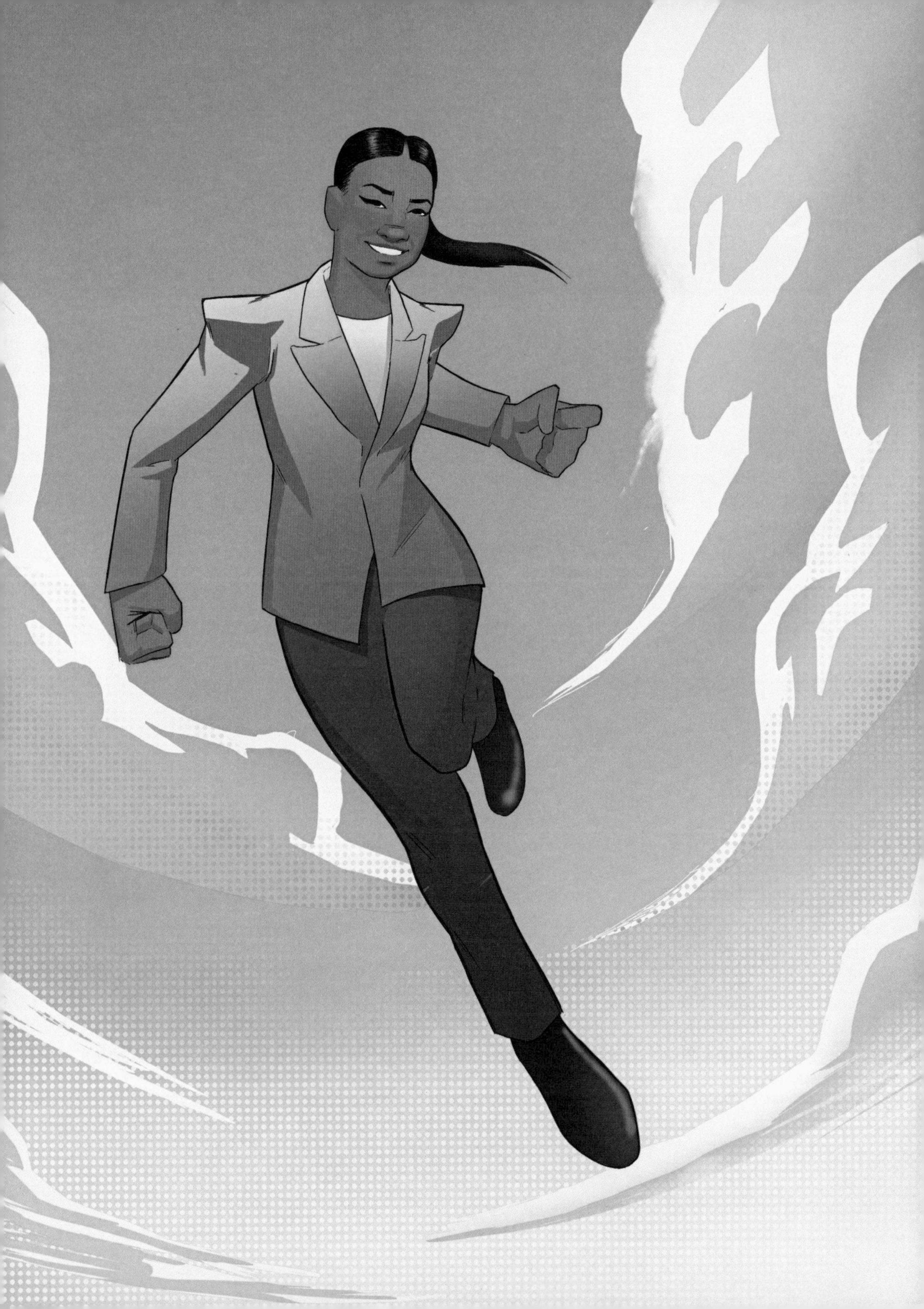

ENGLAND TEAM

POWER
Football

TOOL
Unity

The sun stands still in the sky in anticipation. The wind takes a deep inhale and holds the world's breath. The moon waits, and the ground beneath the football pitch begins to break. Grass and mud fly everywhere, and spectators leap to their feet as fireworks shoot from the lights of the stadium. Emerging from the earth, and from several Premier League teams, the Mighty Miracles rise with golden balls under their feet and balled fists on their hips. The roar from the crowd can be heard from London to Lisbon and Lebanon to Lagos.

From the centre of the pitch emerges Reading's daring Danielle Carter, Brighton's relentless Rinsola Babajide, Bristol's electric Ebony Salmon, Chelsea's dominating Drew Spence, Aston Villa's amazing Anita Asante and Manchester United's leading lady, Lauren James. Lights spark from them as the podium they stand upon commands the attention of the sun, the wind and even the moon, who cannot bear to miss the joining of this black dream team to represent England's football 'club'.

Packed with the tricks and trophies they have taught and won at different corners of the earth, and coming together to break ground and electrify the entire atmosphere, these Avengers weave in and out of each other on the pitch like a dance. The palms of the people watching grow hot with applause, for this performance is like nothing anyone has ever seen.

The power of this many black women moving in unison, in one team, stops the world in its tracks. 'What a performance!' whispers the wind.

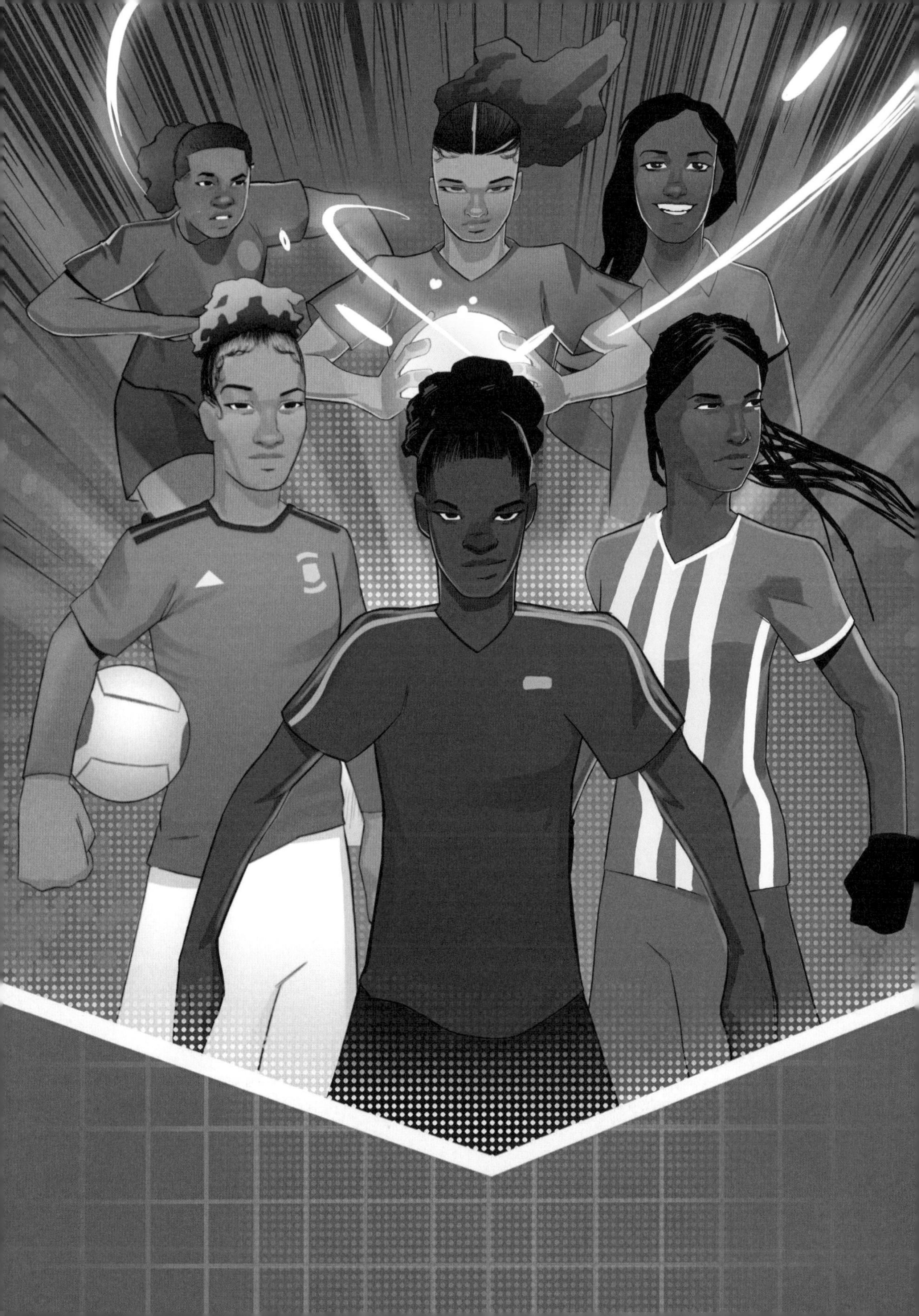

PROF. FRANK CHINEGWUNDOH MBE

POWER
Reading the human body

TOOL
Researching

Whilst other kids would fuss over the things that their bodies could not do, Frank Chinegwundoh would marvel at the possibilities of what could be done. Where most saw a finish line, Frank saw a start line. With two feet on the track and a stethoscope in hand, he would activate his medical tools then adventure through the human body's potential.

Professor Frank Chinegwundoh launched from a good grammar school to medical school at St George's, University of London, where he was one of only two black students in his year. His presence as a black man in a mostly white space was always brought to his attention. Whether it was being advised to change his name to something more 'English', or even being rejected from roles that he was made to occupy, he has never been allowed to forget the colour of his skin. So, along with the medical equipment, it became a big part of his powers.

Professor Frank Chinegwundoh understood that, if there were only a few black doctors, there was probably a world of specifically black medical problems that were being overlooked. He was right. After travelling in West Africa and gathering statistics on black men, he learnt that they were three times more likely to get prostate cancer than white men. For twenty-five years since, he has made it his mission to save the black man's life. He does this through joining numerous advisory and consultancy boards, publishing countless papers and even chairing the charity Cancer Black Care since 1998.

It is no wonder that his power to see hope where others see the end has earned him an MBE from Her Majesty The Queen.

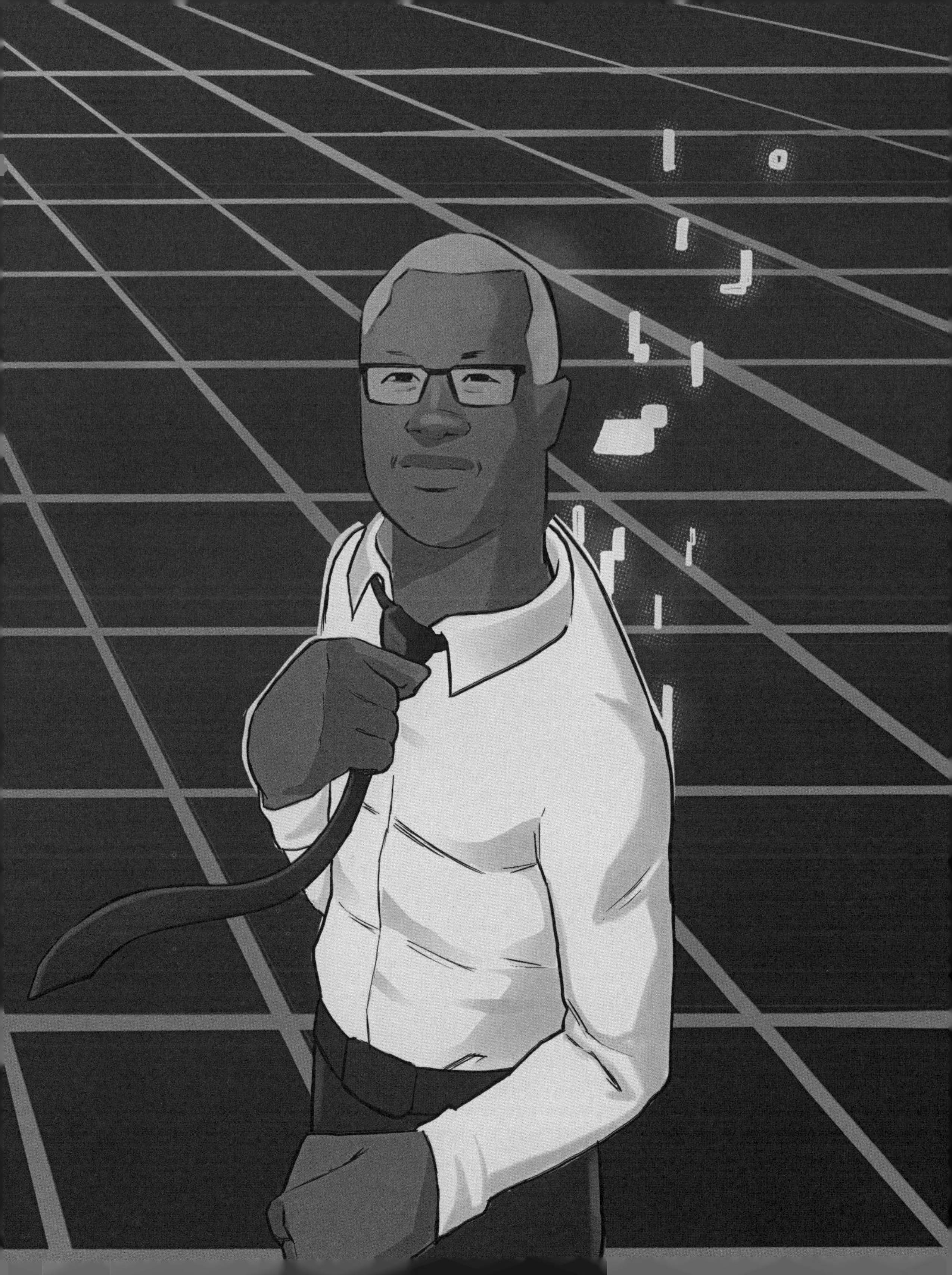

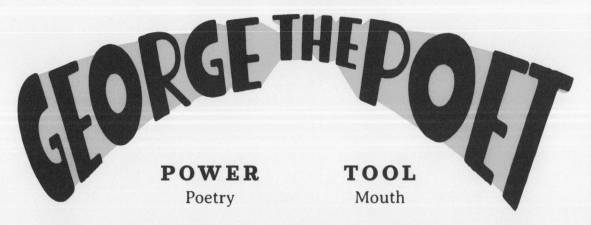

GEORGE THE POET

POWER
Poetry

TOOL
Mouth

Like a puzzle, the pieces of his mind spin around his mouth, slotting in and out of each other, eager to find a pattern that rhymes. And when it does, oh the poetry! The paintings that George the Poet's thoughts become through his mouth are nothing short of verbal masterpieces. Impatiently, these strings of sentences twist and spin behind his lips, counting down the seconds, beats and bars until they are allowed to shoot from George's mouth into microphones at the royal palaces, the BBC and hundreds of other global stages. From Coca-Cola campaigns to podcasts, George's patterns put a spell on every ear they land in.

Poetry is not where his powers first found their feet. Whilst attending Queen Elizabeth's High School for Boys, his brain filled with more and more information about the world, and George couldn't help but notice that there was a deadly imbalance between people with different incomes and skin colours. The world's rage bubbled inside his mouth, eventually spilling out as rap. His rapping caught the attention of musicians and change-makers alike, all wowed by how eloquently he could dismantle and explore society through verse. In time, and as more information filled his mind, George's patterns became more complex, lengthy and creative. They needed more space. They needed a new genre: spoken word.

With this new freedom heavy on his tongue, he has gone on to become the face of social justice, poetry and storytelling, winning a Peabody award for his groundbreaking podcast *'Have You Heard George's Podcast?'*

When we don't quite know how to explain our frustration with the world, George lends us his mind and mouth.

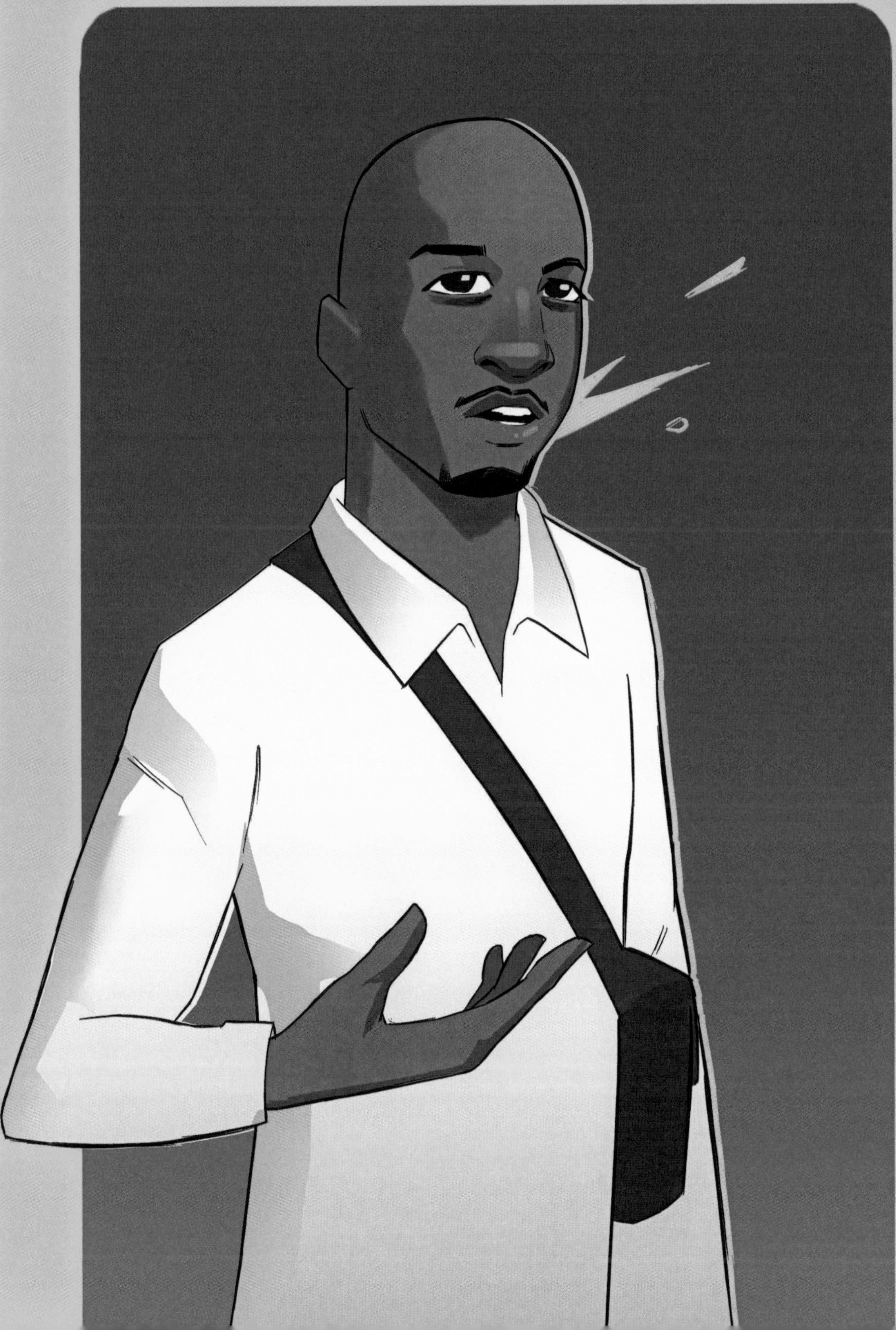

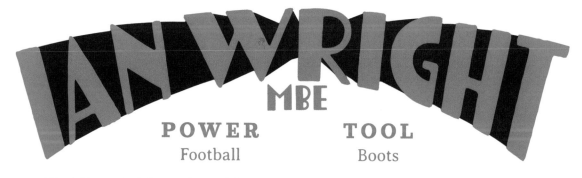

IAN WRIGHT MBE

POWER
Football

TOOL
Boots

'God,' he cried from the cold concrete floor of a short-stay jail cell, 'if you let me out, I'll do everything I can to harness the power within me.' As the bars were pulled apart, the future looked brighter than it ever had for Ian Wright. He had made a promise to God to give his all — to provide for his child and turn his life into something more than a stereotype. Ian stepped out of his trainers to put on his new boots. Not the old ones that did not seem to bring out the best in him, but these new hungry boots, which were shaking in the box, eager to surround the feet of this footballer. As he slid them on, they carried him from Sunday league football to Crystal Palace, where he scored 117 goals and earned the title 'Player of the Century'.

Together with his new boots and promise, Ian Wright went on to wow the wider world, pulling Arsenal, West Ham and even England to victory over and over. As time went on and his new boots trusted Ian with even more power, Wright got faster, more skilful and more passionate about the game. The power had overtaken his whole body and on the pitch he was explosive, becoming England's top division's highest goal-scorer for a season. As the years of football filled Ian's body, he became so heavy with experience and insight that he needed another stadium. One that would let him sit down and release his power in a different way. The power that had made a home of his body was making such an impact on the globe that only a book could capture this excellence and insight into the beautiful game that he was still playing for Arsenal. He gave us his autobiography *Mr Wright*, a bite into his brilliance. A brilliance that, even after hanging up those special boots for the last time, could not be contained.

He became one of football's finest pundits, sharing the minds of players on the pitch and helping fans understand the final score. He brought his unique insights to BBC's *Match of the Day*, ITV and countless post-game interviews. For this, and much more, Wright was awarded an MBE in 2000 and inducted into the National Football Museum Hall of Fame in 2005.

Ian Wright is evidence of God keeping his promise to use football to change lives.

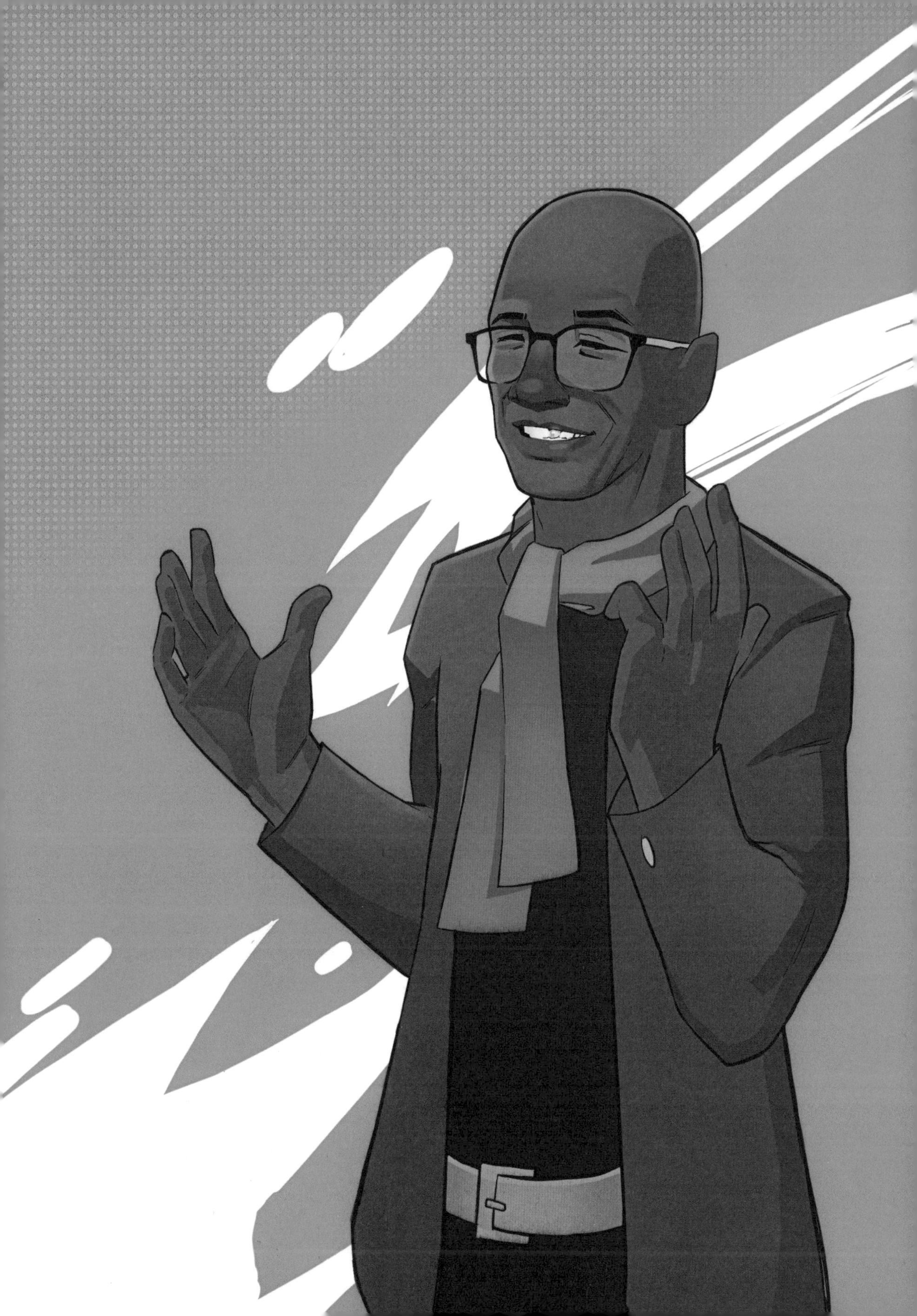

IKRAM ABDI OMAR

POWER
Hijab

TOOL
Modesty

It was always everywhere. It was in the henna that decorated her aunties' arms like flowers climbing up the wall of a palace that only her prince could enter. It was in the intricate designs that wrapped her Somali aunties in the most beautifully modest dresses. It was in the colourful celebrations of Eid and all of the family photos. Fashion and expression have circled around Ikram Abdi Omar since the day she was born in Sweden. As a child, she soaked in how stunning modesty could be, how beautiful a hijab was once draped around the made-up faces of her mother and aunties. The world sees hijabs as a way to hide beauty, but really they are a sign of it, and, in her twenties, Ikram Abdi Omar finally got a chance to show the world what she had always known to be true. Whilst browsing Bristol's Cabot Circus shopping centre, a casting director recognised the beauty and vision in Ikram. There was something in how powerful she became whilst in her hijab that caught their eye, and later, the eyes of the world. Despite initial worry from her family, Ikram pursued modelling full time. Her power, the one that wraps around her breathtaking face, graced the cover of *Vogue Arabia* and she became the first UK hijabi to ever do so — opening up the door for many Muslim women to realise that fashion and religion can co-exist everywhere from family gatherings to the Burberry campaign of 2019 or a runway with Naomi Campbell walking for Tommy Hilfiger. Ikram Abdi Omar protects a 'my rules' section of all of her contracts to ensure that her Muslim boundaries are honoured.

In an industry built on beautiful faces, Ikram reveals the beauty in so much more.

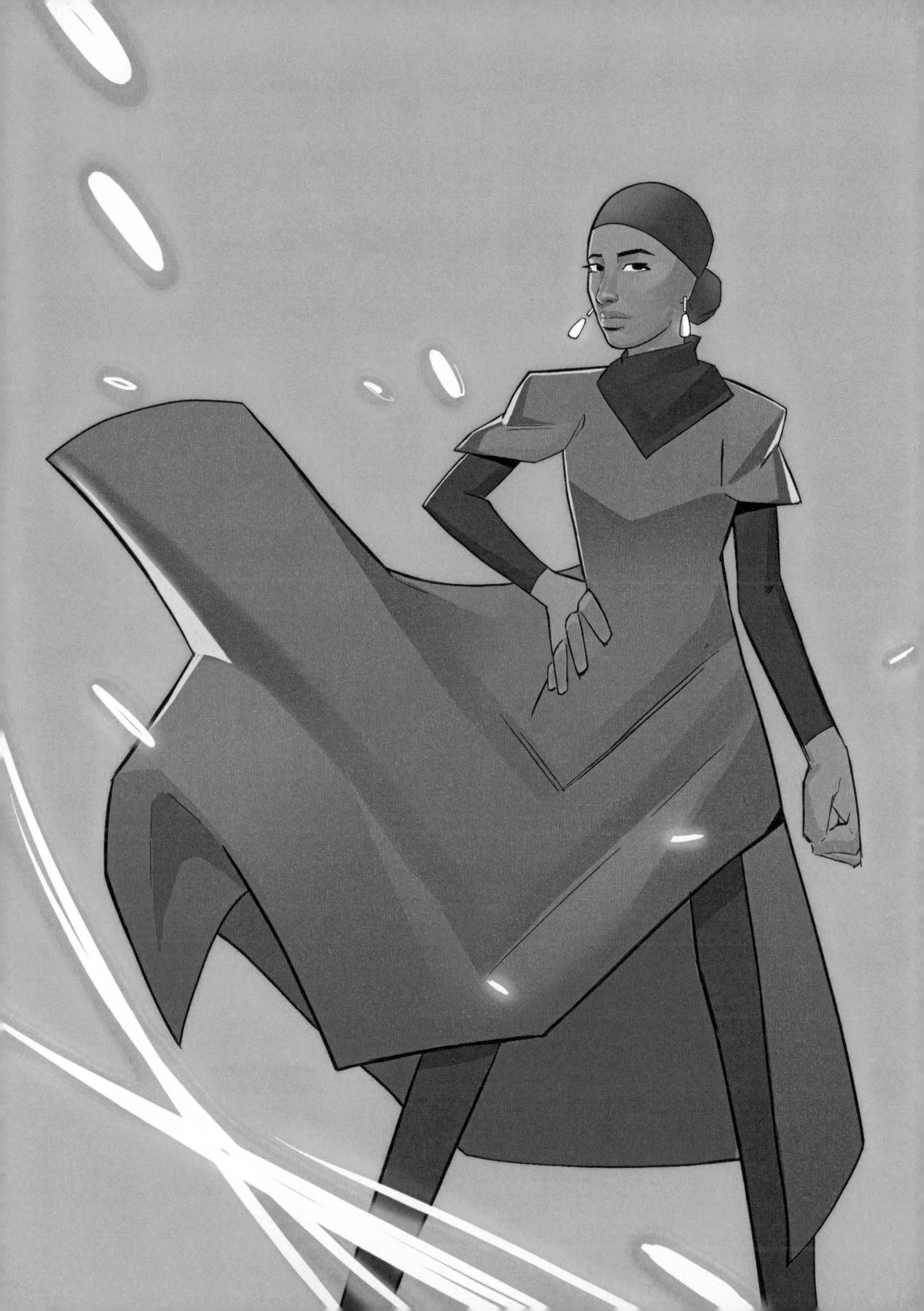

INUA ELLAMS

POWER
Palms of poetry

TOOL
Plays

He might have left Nigeria, but Nigeria never left him. Home circles above his head like a halo, spilling its lessons and teachings down into everything that Inua Ellams creates with his paintbrush hands. A spiderweb of colour and culture forms around the writer, connecting, disconnecting and discovering the many ways that blackness and Africanness can print on a new land. He rubs his palms into poetry and plays, dusting the mix of his experiences in Nigeria and London onto various award-winning pages. The stories and images dance off the canvas to live in audience members' hearts and minds as pieces of time gifted to them by Inua. He has serenaded the world over and over again with his words that land like both a kiss and a kick. Depending on which of the four poetry books you let yourself become enchanted by, you might adventure into his mystical mind to find pieces of his past tucked between lyrical rhymes and rhythms. But Inua doesn't believe in entirely surrendering to readers' interpretations. Some poems just have to be given a body to wear and a stage to perform on. He created R.A.P Party events to give poems and poets a chance to find their mouths and movement. Performance poetry is the bridge towards his strongest tool: plays. Inua Ellams has repeatedly coloured the white face of theatre. He has seasoned the scene with award-winning, sold-out plays that tell tales of identity. *Barber Shop Chronicles* pulls the entire universe into a room for one hour and forty-five minutes. Inua's play not only sold out every night at the National Theatre, but went on to tour the world.

He places his poetic palms around hearts and captures them perfectly.

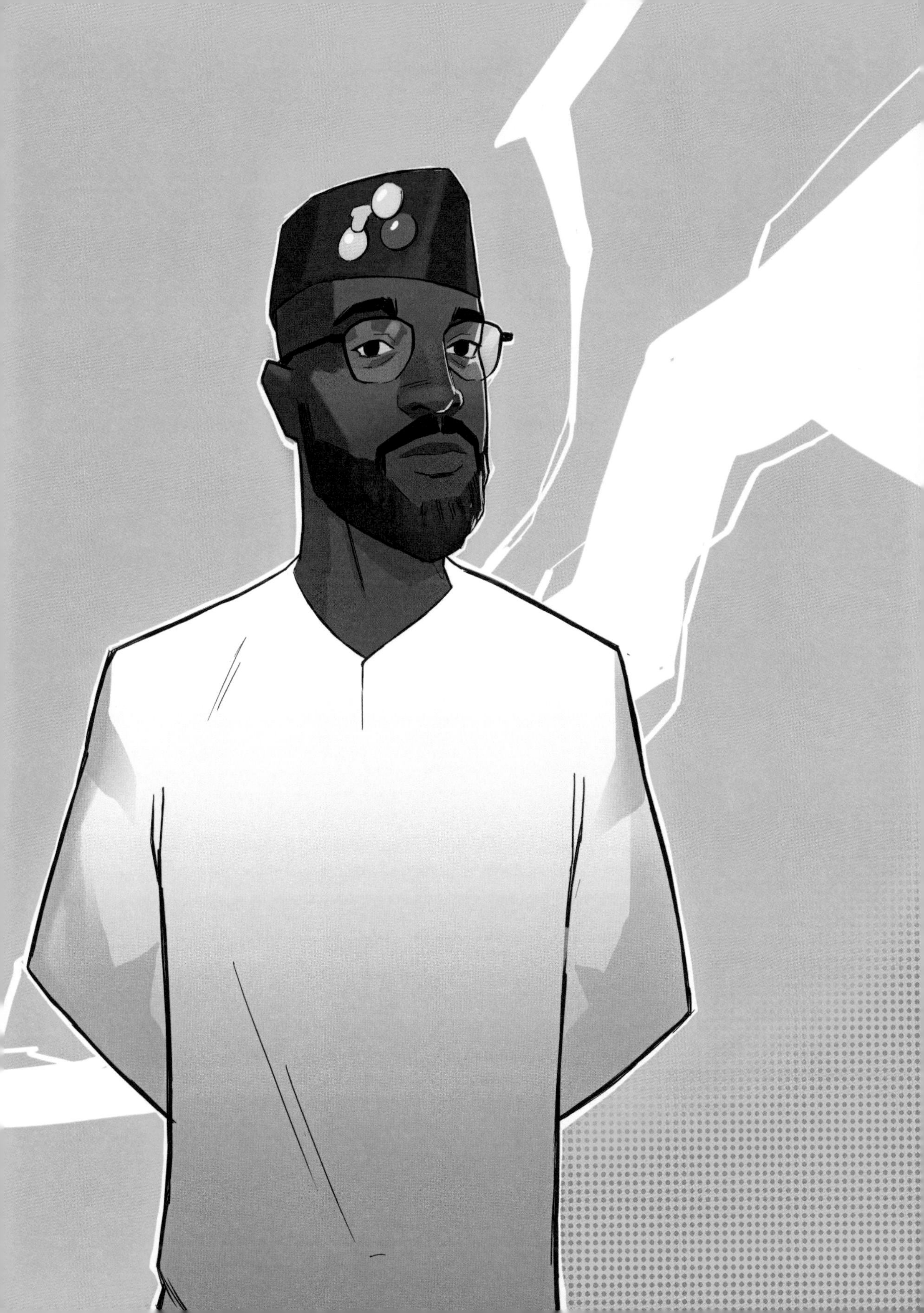

JORDAN JARRETT-BRYAN

POWER
Basketball

TOOL
Magic leg

As the connection is made, sparks fly from the leg of Jordan Jarrett-Bryan, bonding metal to flesh, fantasy to reality, the power to the person. Whilst the bond is being made, the stars above shake in the arms of the sky, drawing out a new pattern for the sportsman with one prosthetic leg. The metal pieces release threads that travel through Jordan's sleeping body, weaving a new future into his life. As the threads from his new artificial leg reach his brain, they deposit the confidence and extreme focus that will be needed to maintain his powers. Although he wakes up slowly and carefully, when once he shakes off the anaesthetic and gets used to his new movement, Jordan Jarrett-Bryan launches into his new life like a fish to water.

He channelled and trained the powerful threads that pulsed through his body to play wheelchair basketball. And he got pretty good at it too! Bryan played for twenty years at club and national level. His mesmerising ability to wield his power with speed and precision impressed everybody on and off the court. Jordan became the captain of the Men's Great Britain Junior wheelchair basketball team, and led them to win two European championships. His relationship with his new body took him from South London to Italy, to play professionally again and win yet another championship. After accomplishing such incredible achievements in basketball, he took on another piece of metal . . . the microphone! Jordan began presenting, and the confidence that was sewn into him as a boy oozed out onto Channel 4 and the Premier League productions, where he took up sports reporting.

Jordan Jarrett-Bryan continues to show the world that not having one limb just makes space for a new power to be built into the human body.

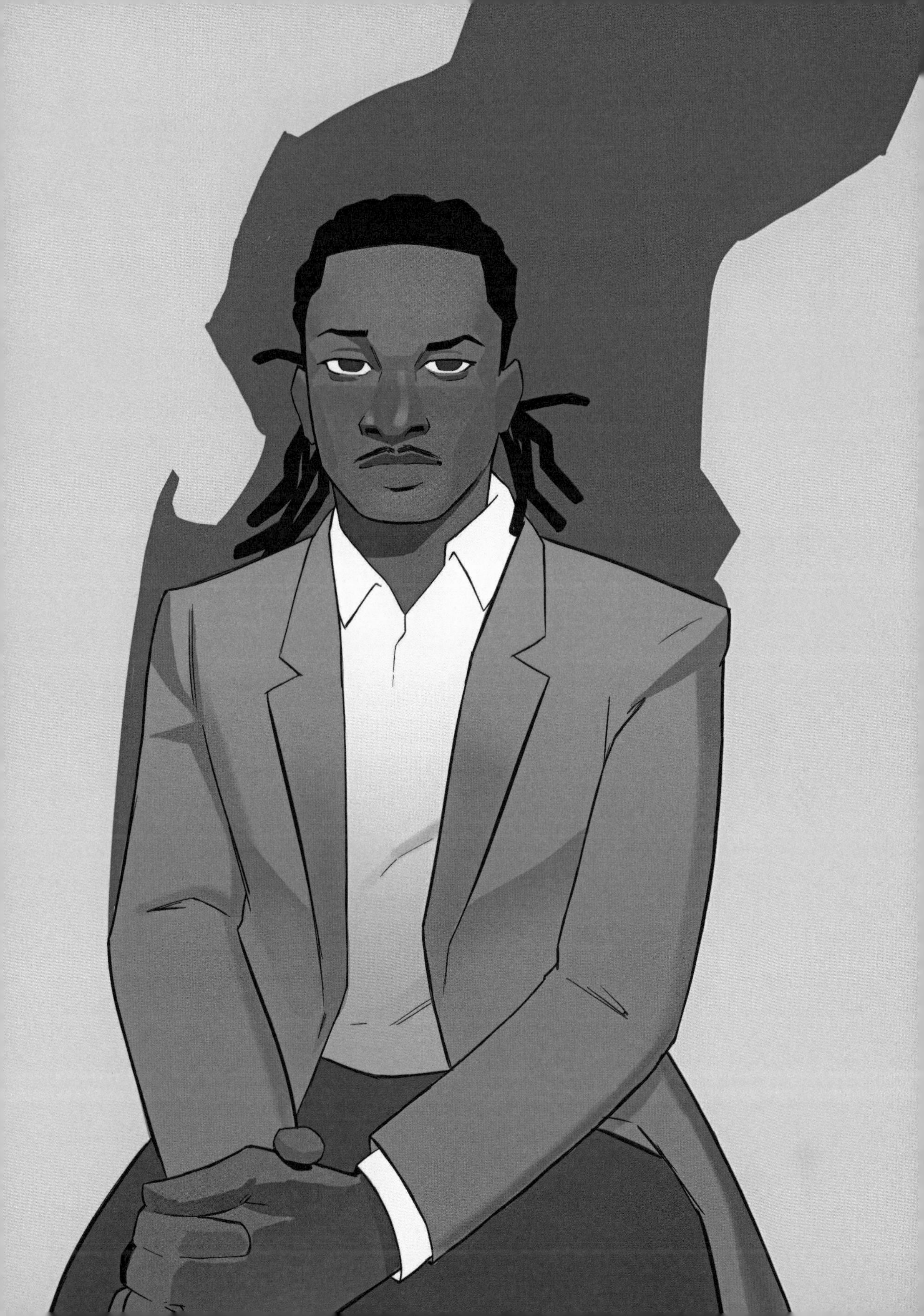

JOSHUA BUATSI

POWER
Boxing

TOOL
The Bible

The third home, where the trinity intertwines. Where Ghana crashes into Croydon and Croydon swaps flip-flops for boxing boots. Destiny is sealed together by a mother's prayer to protect and guide her son to victory. When Joshua Buatsi bows his head, standing in the centre of the ring with balled fists, he detonates the power within him with a verse from the Bible. From the inside out, confidence, faith and speed ignite within his veins and tear through his body, causing a brilliant glow to penetrate his skin. The spectators mistake it for sweat until they witness the radiating power in action at the Copper Box, where Buatsi collects his title as British Light-Heavyweight. It is then the world realises that he holds the 'God glow', the one he trains for by praying just as much as through his sport.

At the core of a people-centred industry, Buatsi freezes the world by shifting the focus from him to his coach: God.

'It is God who trains my hands for war and my fingers for battle.'

As in the story of David and Goliath, Joshua Buatsi is not to be undermined. He sharpens his power by studying the giants around him, such as Anthony Joshua. Buatsi insists that learning is a vital aspect of his time in the ring. Studying how his opponent moves and fights feeds the strategy that strengthens his spirit. The spirit that never forgets — 2 Timothy 1:7.

'For God has not given us a spirit of fear, but of power.'

50

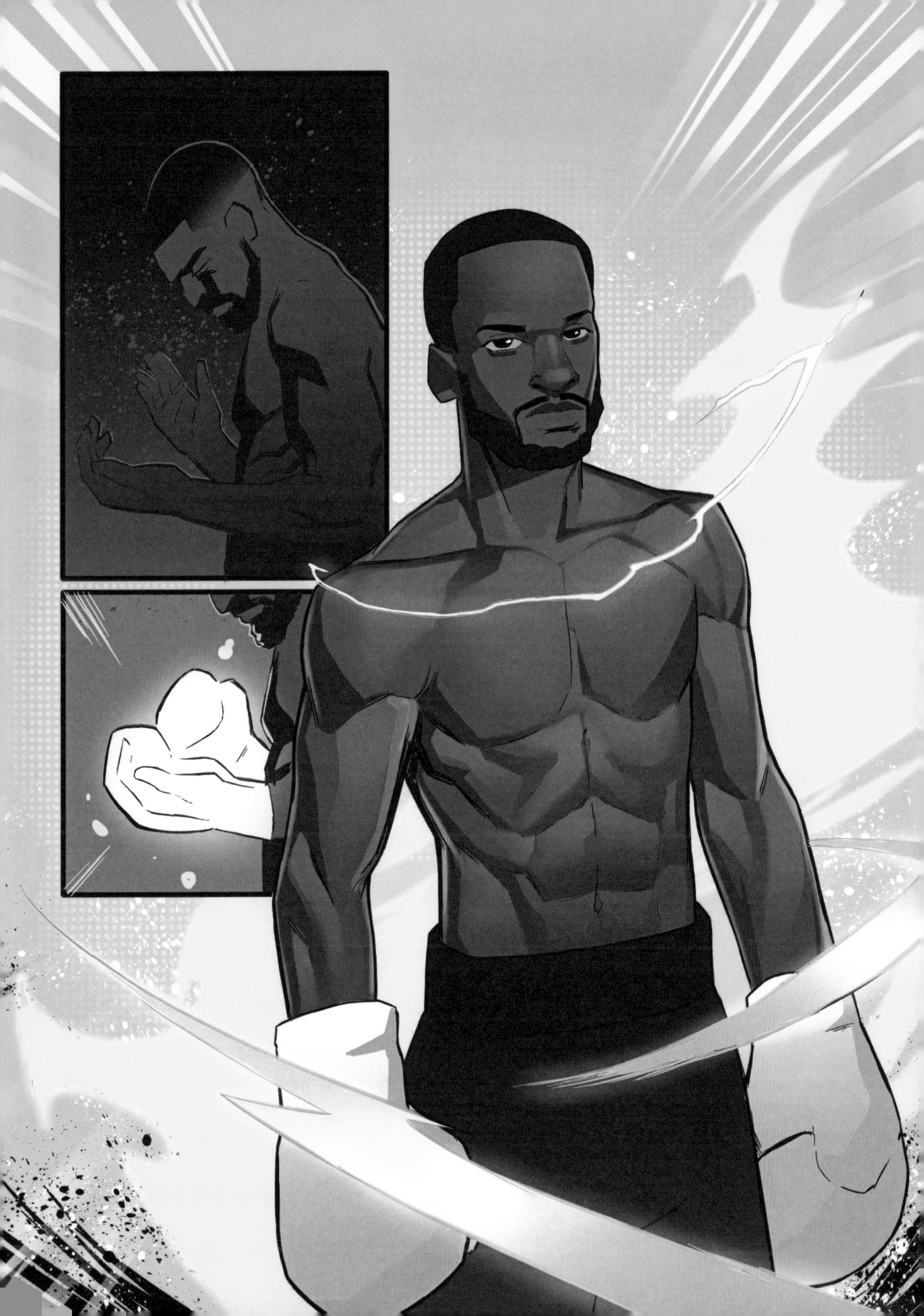

JOURDAN DUNN

POWER
Modelling

TOOL
Fashion

The spotlights flickered in anticipation. The nervous pulse of the catwalk could be felt throughout New York. The camera operators fidgeted nervously, busying their fingers whilst they patiently waited for the coming of a new supermodel. Finally, the day had arrived. The world of fashion held its breath as fourteen-year-old Jourdan Dunn and her friends stepped into Primark.

Although the next few minutes had already been sketched in the stars for decades, Jourdan was unaware of how life-changing this trip to Primark would be. Blissfully, she tried on glasses and posed for the mirror, attracting the crucial part of her future, like a magnet. As the model scout observed from the shadows, they saw the future flash before their eyes. In a sharp second, their mind was filled with images of this teenage girl on the covers of *Vogue*, *Elle*, *Glamour*, *Wonderland* and commanding a global audience on the luxury fashion runway. And so the story goes . . . Jourdan Dunn was welcomed onto her first runway in New York. The dresses adored being worn by the beautiful, black model. From Prada to Balmain, the clothing lines became obsessed with her style. And so did fifty-six magazine covers and fifty-seven fashion and beauty campaigns!

Flashes erupt from every corner of the runway, photographers hoping to get the perfect picture. Unfortunately for some troubled onlookers, the picture can only be perfect if the skin is white. Jourdan has had to defend her colour, culture and hair in an industry of vultures time and time again.

But her black remains beautiful and worth millions more than any amount of racism.

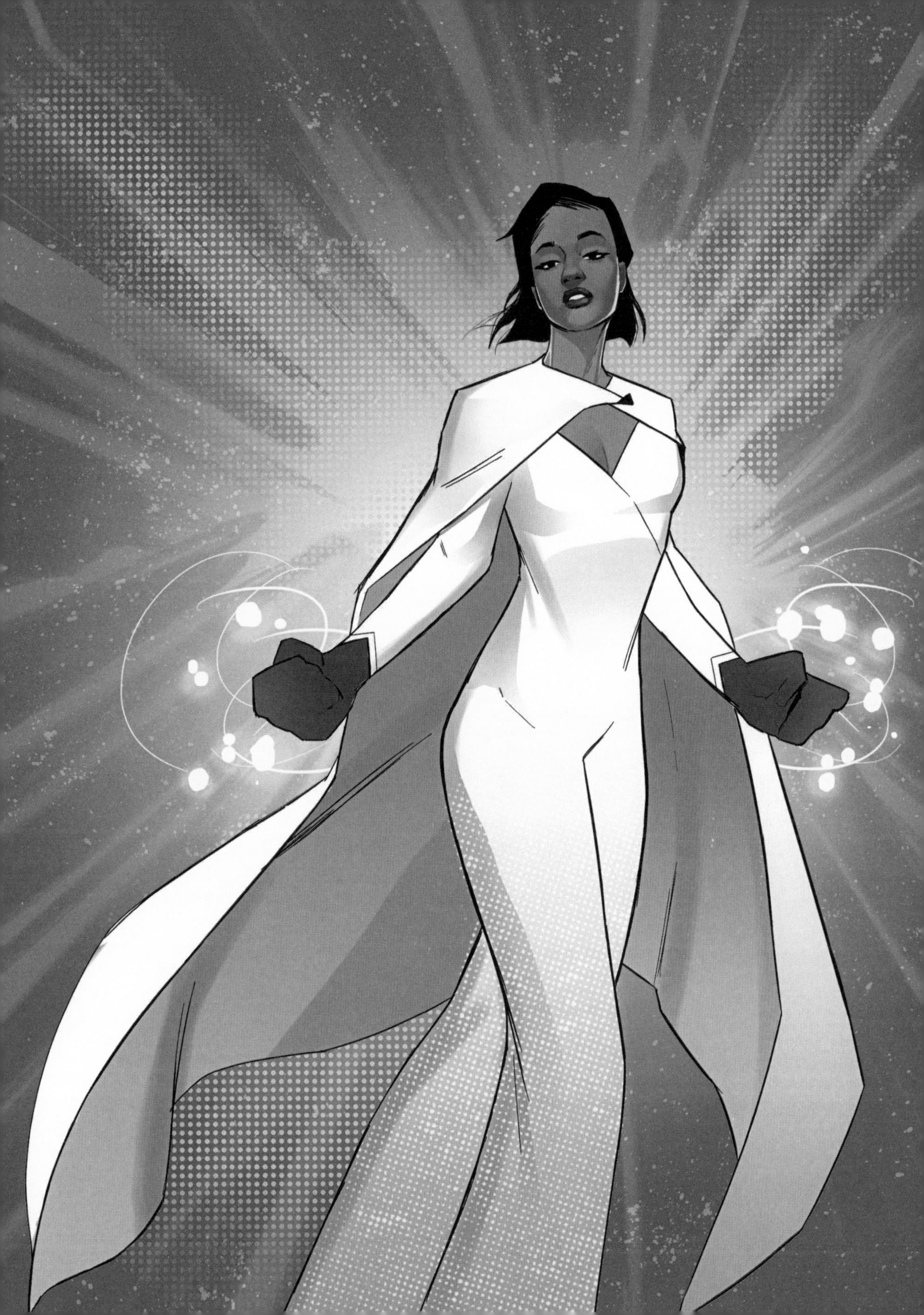

KATARINA JOHNSON-THOMPSON

POWER
Heptathlon

TOOL
Power blending

In a frenzy, though Katarina walks slowly towards the athletics track for the first time, it zaps around her body at lightning speed, trying to fill as many of Katarina Johnson-Thompson's limbs as possible. Super strength and gravity clash like titans in her legs, desperate to occupy her lower body. Flexibility and power chase each other around her hips like a charge in an electric circuit, extending to all possible points. Oblivious to the battle zone inside her body, the second Katarina Johnson-Thompson's foot steps onto the athletics track, a ground-breaking eruption occurs inside her and the different superpowers burst around her body like fireworks, rebounding off her legs to her hips to her hands, intertwining into a new ultra power.

Dame Jessica Ennis-Hill had spent years mastering the art of making different powers dance together. In time, Katarina Johnson-Thompson learnt this too — she even went on to break Ennis-Hill's heptathlon record.

Heptathlon athletes are trained to excel in every sport on the track, from running to jumping to throwing. Johnson-Thompson's excellence was evident at the 2019 World Championships, where she broke the British record and won gold. And in 2012 where all of her powers gathered in her legs to launch her onto the podium as the world junior champion.

Every time Katarina takes that step onto the track, her powers join hands and break out one by one, at the perfect time.

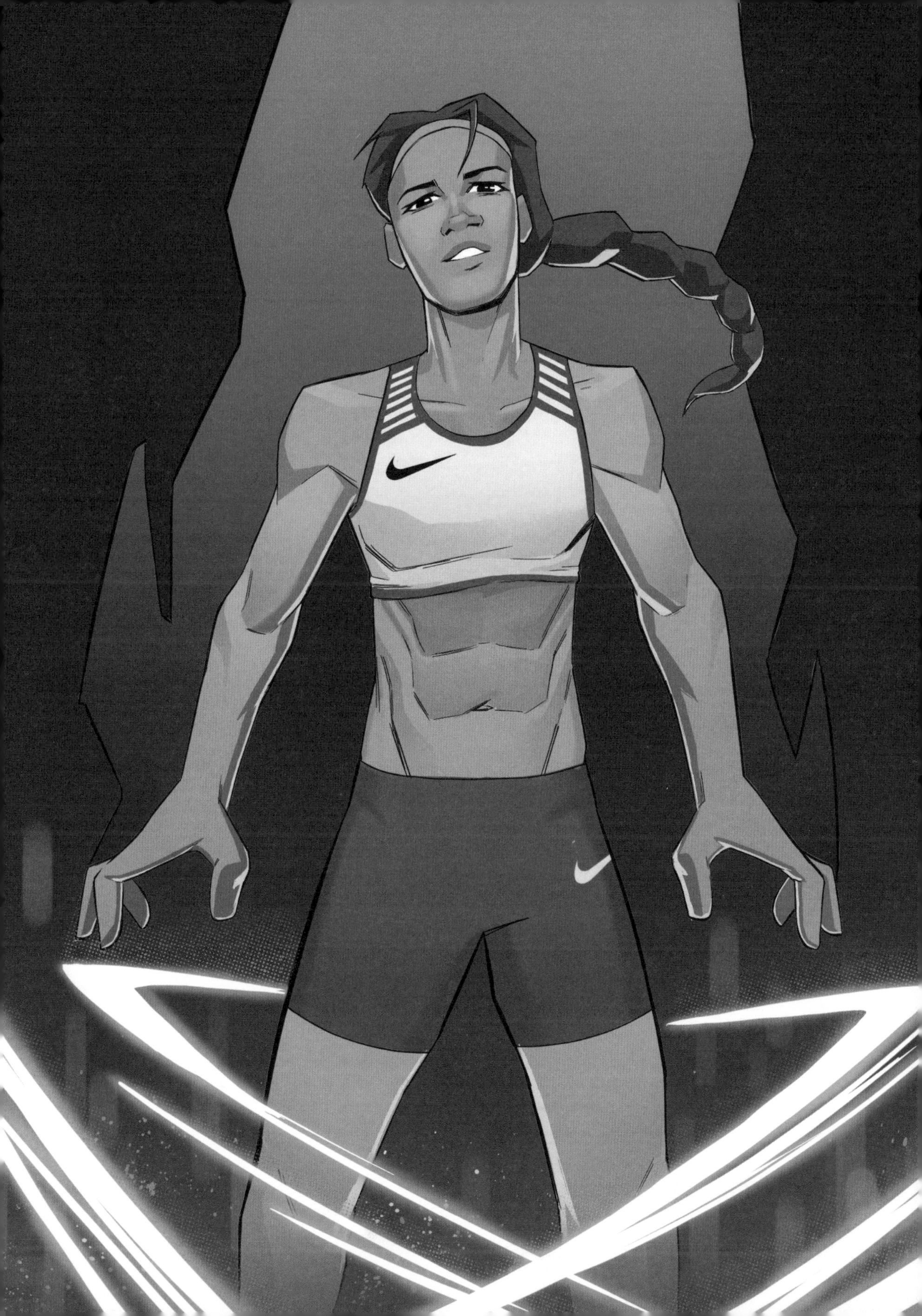

KOSAR ALI

POWER
Acting

TOOL
Friendship

Friendship is vital in every story — but especially in Kosar Ali's. In the presence of her best friends, she grows powerful wings of confidence, energising encouragement and super support, which help her fly into the various minds of many different characters.

Although Kosar's ability to step into the mind and body of any character began to show in primary school, she never considered herself an actor until the day finally came for her gift to explode within her — with the support of her best friends cheering her on! The day the crew of *Rocks* walked into Kosar's school and set up a workshop for students to explore the characters in the film, was the day that Sumaya was born. This character had been waiting in the belly of Kosar Ali — vibrant and bold — with friendship at the core of her. Friendship was the thread that connected Kosar to Sumaya, and to the entire *Rocks* cast who were all empowered by its support. So much so that parts of *Rocks* were improvised, but it was still award-winning for its authenticity and emotive acting.

Kosar Ali walked away BIFA award-winning and BAFTA nominated from her performance in *Rocks*. She also left with new and powerful friendship bonds that continue to support her excellence.

Kosar reminds us that individually we can be great, but together we become powerful.

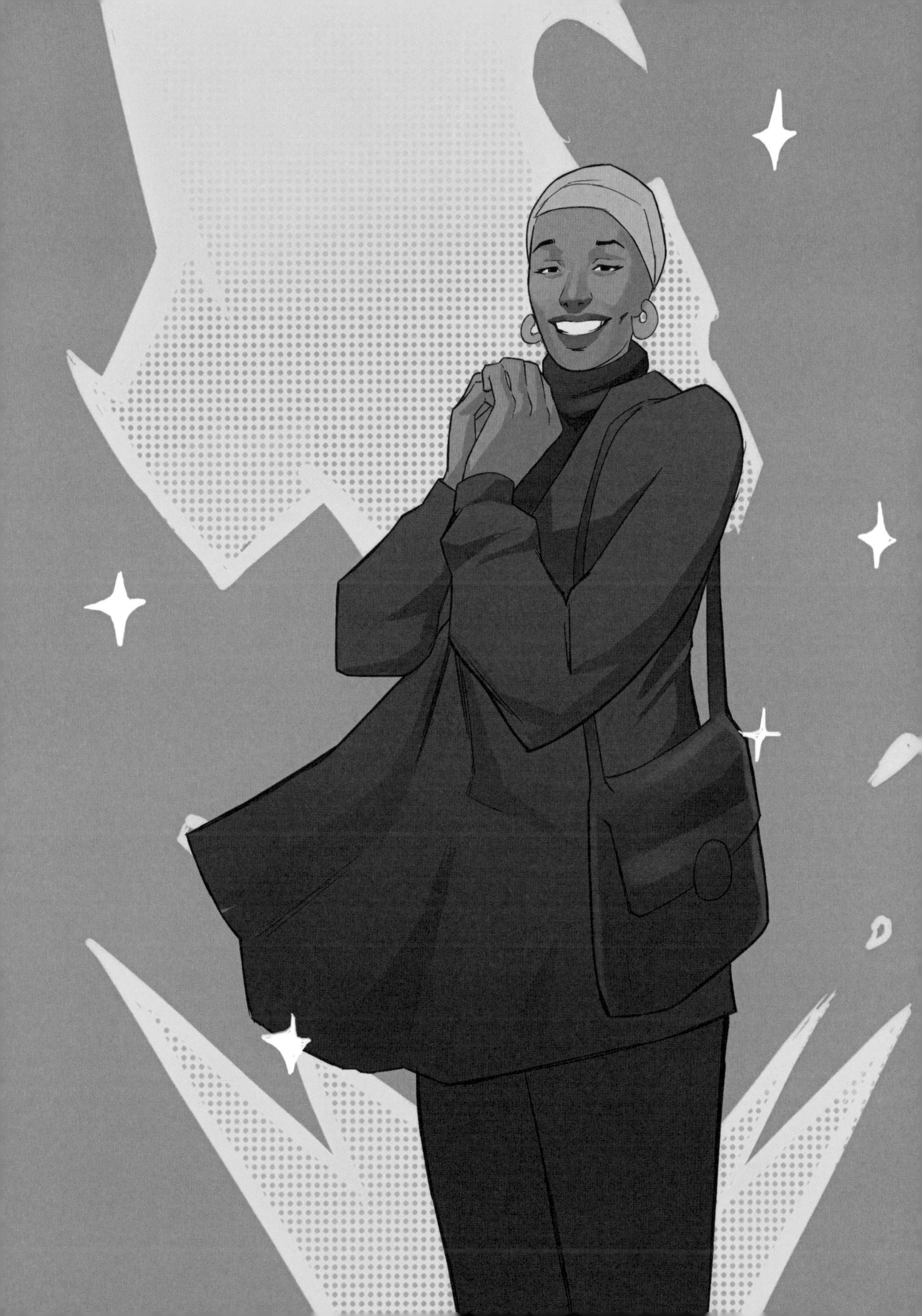

LEOMIE ANDERSON

POWER
Modelling

TOOL
Fashion

The runways waited. The cameras held their breath. The make-up artists readied their stations, and the hairdressers had their combs and gels on standby, eagerly anticipating the transformation of a pavement in South West London.

At fourteen years old, Leomie Anderson's legs pressed the concrete further and further away, until glitter-filled stages emerged to take its place and the vision of Leomie the supermodel materialised in front of the modelling agent who had been placed there to fulfil Leomie's magazine destiny. The spotlight that shone on her then has not turned off since. It loves her soft but striking features, her wise but gentle knowingness.

Leomie Anderson is her own superpower and has revealed her might on different platforms. Leomie's first show was for Marc Jacobs — then Tom Ford, and then Moschino. Brands that represent quality are attracted to this supermodel. Upon realising this, Leomie launched her own quality superhero clothing range, LAPP, in 2017. It has since gone on to catch eyes in magazines and on posters, allowing girls everywhere to become superheroes too, whether they are following in Leomie's footsteps onto the TEDx stage, or studying in the top universities in the countries that she has visited.

Leomie Anderson releases her light into the world to shine on others and encourage them to love how they sparkle in their own mirrors.

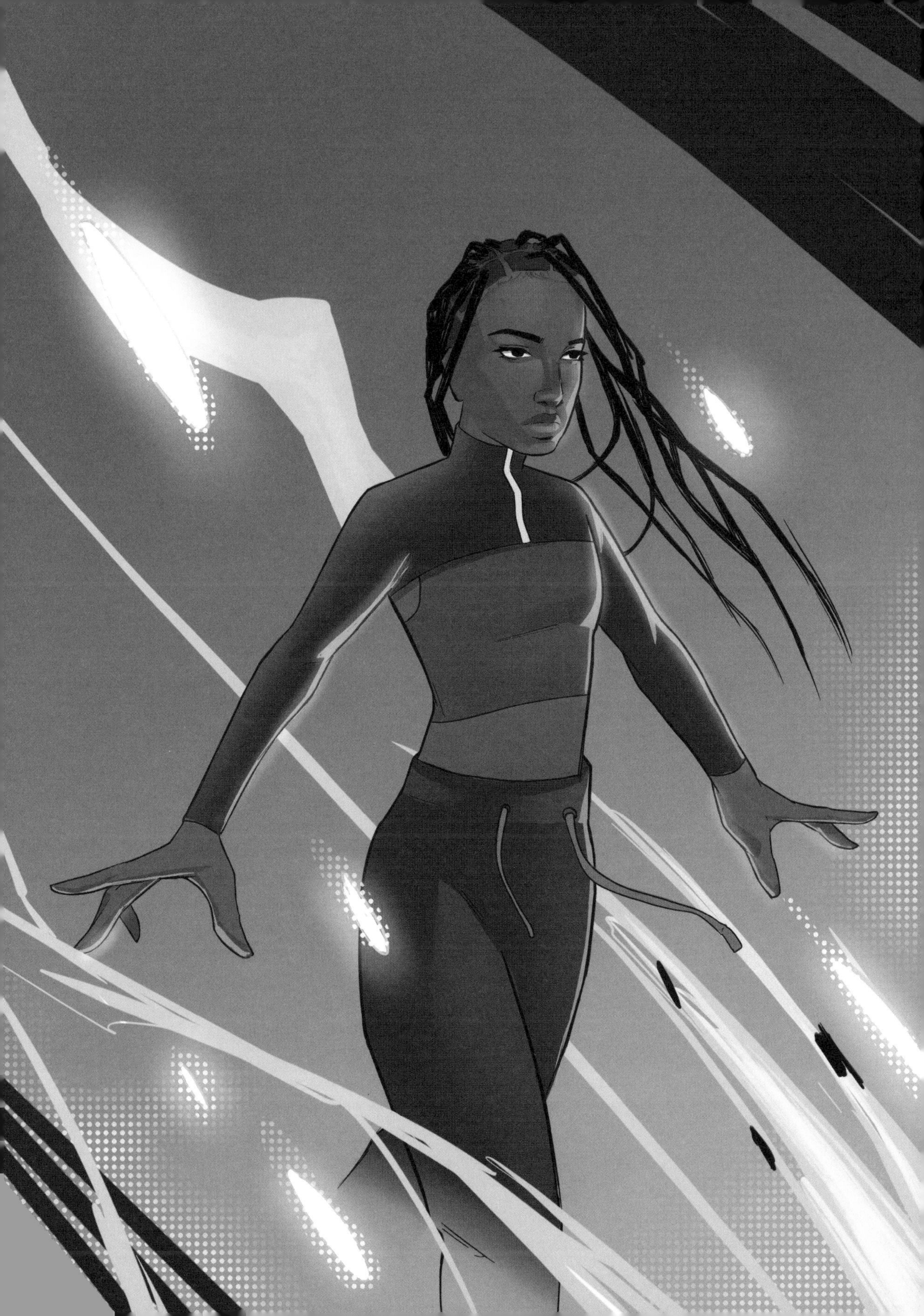

POWER
Baking

TOOL
Oven

As the dough rose into its final form and the scent of freshly baked pie escaped the oven, young Liam Charles became enchanted by the smell. His body gave in to it, and the wiring of his senses rerouted to form brand-new connections, permanently linking his heightened senses of smell, taste and touch — the tools needed to finally transform Liam Charles into the baker the world knows today as Cake Boy.

Once senses were connected, the world began to smell, taste and feel very different to Cake Boy. He would eat a pie and his tongue would burst into action, working out which ingredients had been used to create the taste absorbing into his tongue. Over time, he put his senses to delicious use, becoming one with the oven. His unique culinary skills persuaded his teacher to let him hold a bake sale in school. After two sell-out sales, it was confirmed: Cake Boy needed to take things to the next level. His mother's Caribbean kitchen could no longer contain his power. He needed a new laboratory, and *The Great British Bake-Off* kitchen was the perfect fit. For eight weeks, Britain was charmed and obsessed with Cake Boy. So much so that he had to write down his genius baking methods across two books: *Cheeky Treats: Brilliant Bakes and Cakes* and *Second Helpings*.

With whisks as hands and icing as breath, Liam Charles introduces mouths everywhere to his magic.

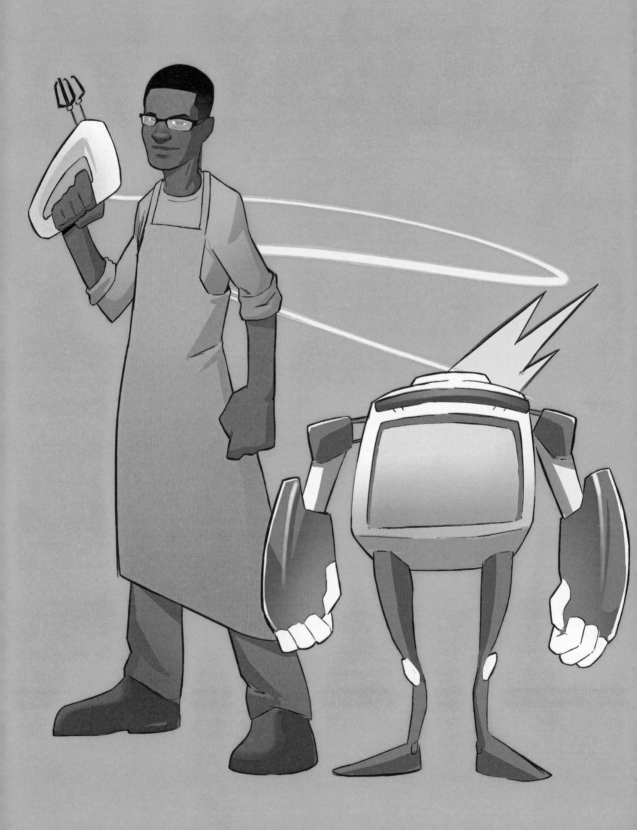

LUOL DENG

POWER
Basketball

TOOL
Ball

As a young boy, Luol Deng jumped from the burnt-orange sands of East Africa into the soft soles of his Jordans — and he hasn't stopped jumping since. Despite his first passion for football, his superpower shines on the basketball court, 3,561 miles away from his birthplace.

When Deng as a child was first passed the ball by his brother, his fingertips left an invisible imprint, and a unique connection was created in his palms, transforming his entire DNA. The connection was transmitted to his wrists, then shot along his arms, chased around his pumping heart, dived down his long spine and landed at his feet, connecting his path to the magnificent game that would change his life forever.

Luol Deng let the sport ignite within him and take control, resulting in two NBA All-Star games and countless buzzer beaters across the world. But no matter how far Deng jumps from home, his proud refugee heart remembers his journey. Luol Deng ensures that the magic that was unlocked in him through a basketball is passed across the globe's courts, empowering every pair of palms that he thrusts his basketball heart into.

His power catches from person to person, palm to palm, igniting an explosion of self-belief and passion in each child that he helps through his foundation.

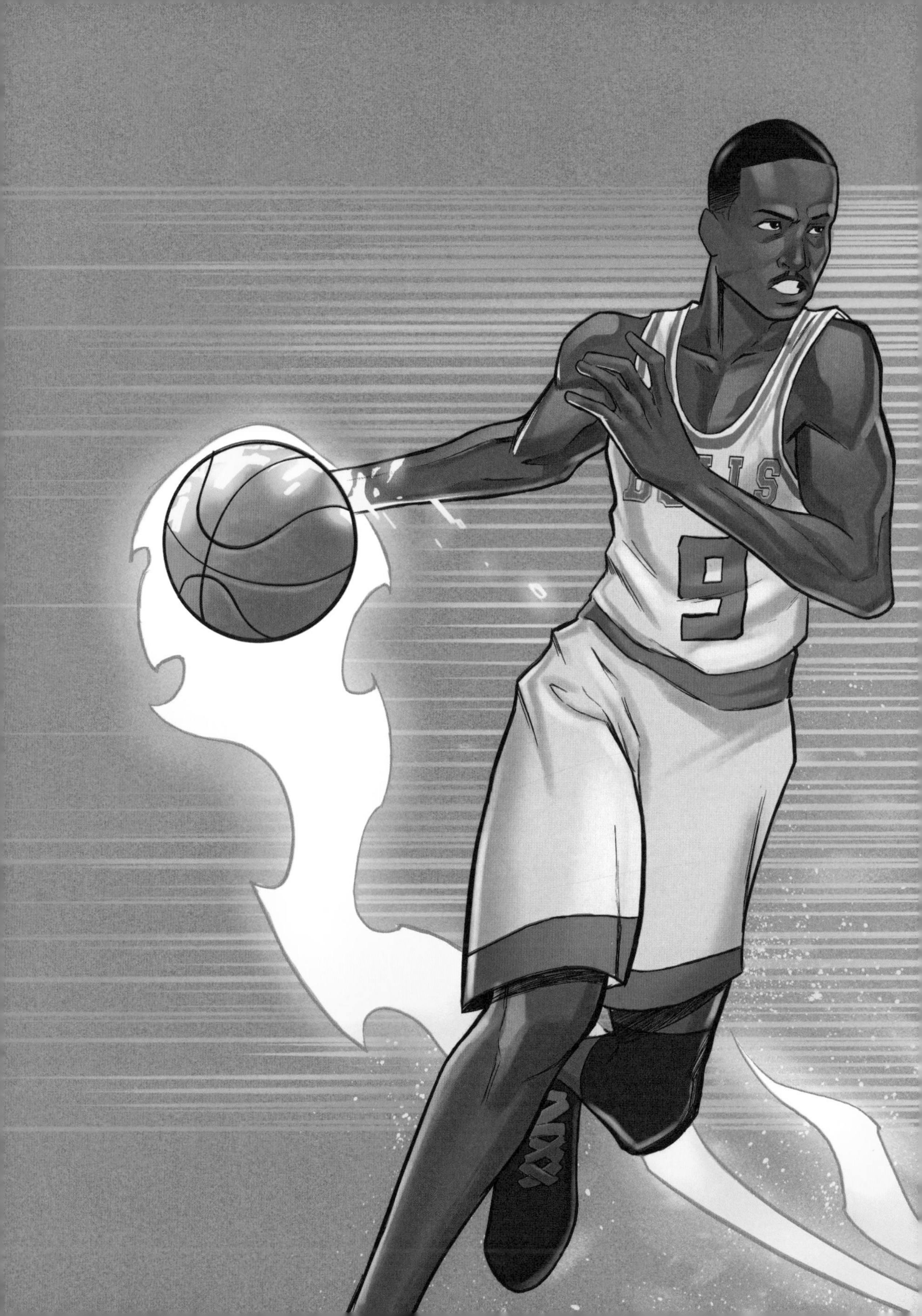
9

DR MARK RICHARDS

POWER
Allowing others to communicate with the sky

TOOL
Sky phone

There was something not quite right in Mark Richards' world. The other students did not realise, but Mark felt the air around him slowly thicken with pollution, and he couldn't understand why nobody else seemed to care. The shift in the atmosphere alarmed young Mark, but he did not know enough about the sky above him to understand what was causing the change. So he began to pay attention in chemistry lessons. The more he learnt about the air, the more he remembered what his mum had been telling him since he was young: 'Education is the passport out of poverty'. To Mark, education was his way to understand what the sky was trying to tell him.

Mark went on to ace chemistry and do a degree at Manchester University, absorbing all the necessary elements to strengthen his communication with the sky. His intimate relationship with the atmosphere meant that he could do what others could not: he built a machine that could detect any harmful chemicals circulating in the air. He then went on to co-found a company that would build more of these machines, allowing others to tap into his conversation with the sky. With a PhD from Imperial College London, Mark Richards has become an expert in talking with the sky.

He lets the people on the ground know what they can do better to cause less pollution.

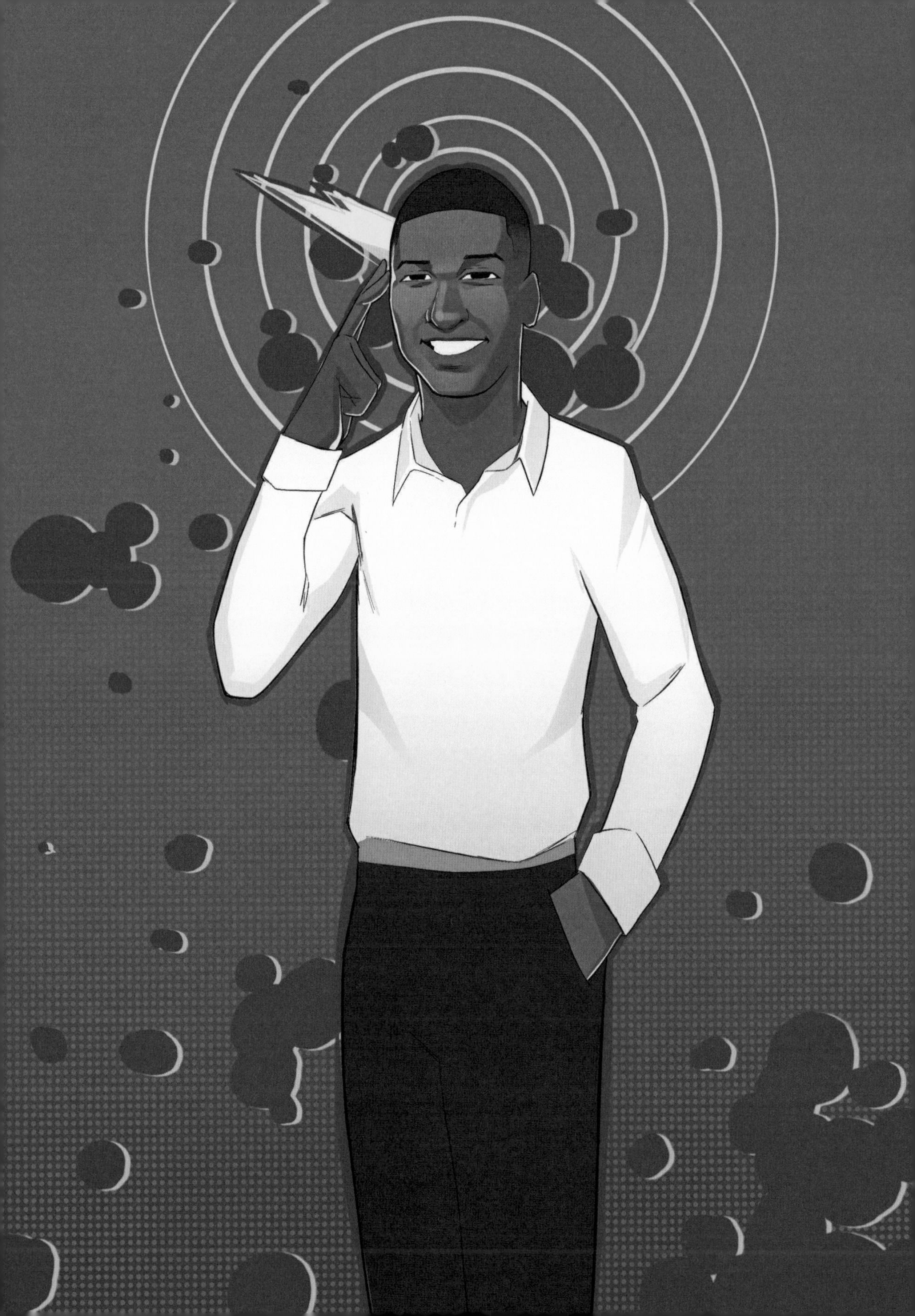

MARO ITOJE

POWER
Rugby

TOOL
His wrists

Rugby is not Maro Itoje's first sport, but it is his finest. Medals have flown and clung to Maro Itoje for as long as he has competed. In athletics, his palms shook with power. The strength of ten stadiums swarmed inside each of his fingertips. And, at the touch of a shot-put, the energy erupted and broke out from his hands, launching the metal ball further than anybody else in England under seventeen.

Although the power in his hands made him excel in multiple sports, from basketball to athletics, his wrists grew impatient. Tucked just beneath each palm was a cylinder box, locking away a current that could only be unleashed by the touch of one specific ball — a rugby ball.

Maro had played rugby since he was eleven, but the boxes in his wrists needed the right environment to break open — this was Harrow School, where his future awaited. After earning a scholarship to the school, the cylinders began to crack slightly on the rugby pitch, pouring just enough current through him to amaze anybody watching him play. He was becoming electrifying on the field. At nineteen, the Saracens finally got hold of Maro and took him under their wing. There, the cylinders finally broke open and filled his entire body.

As time went on, Maro became more comfortable with the current running through him and, after graduating with a degree in politics, he became England's Man of the Match as well as the European Player of the Year in 2016.

Maro Itoje, with a rugby ball in his hand, did what no other young black rugby player has ever done: he scored a try in every Under-20s Six Nations game he played, captained the Under 20s England men's team and in 2017 became the youngest player ever to be selected for a British & Irish Lions' tour to New Zealand. Maro Itoje might have won four English Premiership titles and countless other titles of the highest order, but he has never strayed far from or hidden his Nigerian roots.

The motherland vibrates within him, loud, fashionable and powerful — like art, one of his other passions.

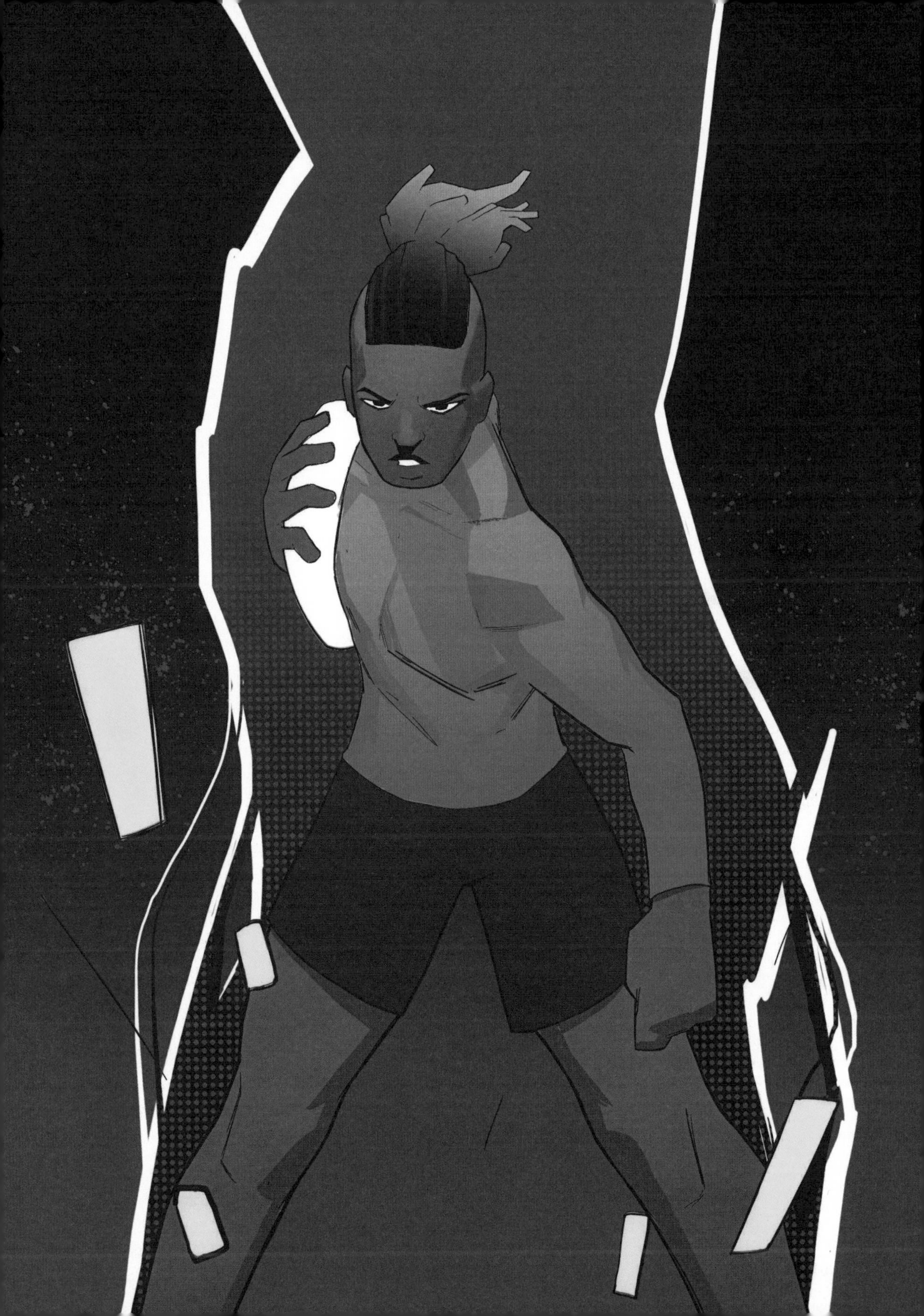

MICHAEL DAPAAH

POWER
Producing

TOOL
Sponge hands

Most people see things for what they are, but few see them for what they could become. Michael Dapaah marvelled over South London. He pondered upon the people within his community, from the Uber drivers to the aspiring rappers. He felt how interesting they truly were. In a moment of inspiration, he stretched his arms out into London and froze time as multiple personalities were absorbed through his sponge hands. Sucking in these people, he became more than the Ghanaian Brunel graduate. So much more. As the various characters of London bubbled inside him, eager to erupt, he rushed home, unlocked his laptop, flicked open his palms and let the various spirits of London spill from his wrists onto YouTube to create the infamous web series *Somewhere in London*. With over 1.9 million subscribers and even more views than his first mockumentary, Dapaah created a global icon — one who would break into the world's speakers, phones, radio stations, brand campaigns, the top three UK music charts and television in a way that had never been done before. Like a grime lullaby being dropped into the world's wind, every corner of the globe came together to recite what became a kind of international anthem.

The ting goes skrrrahh, pap, pap, ka-ka-ka
Skidiki-pap-pap, and a pu-pu-pudrrrr-boom
Skya, du-du-ku-ku-dun-dun

The world became obsessed with Big Shaq, a character created in the loaded palms of Michael Dapaah. A man who not only lets his inspiration leak onto YouTube but also television, social media and, most recently, fitness campaigns.

The weight of the characters that Dapaah absorbs from everyday London keeps him grounded as a champion of everyday people.

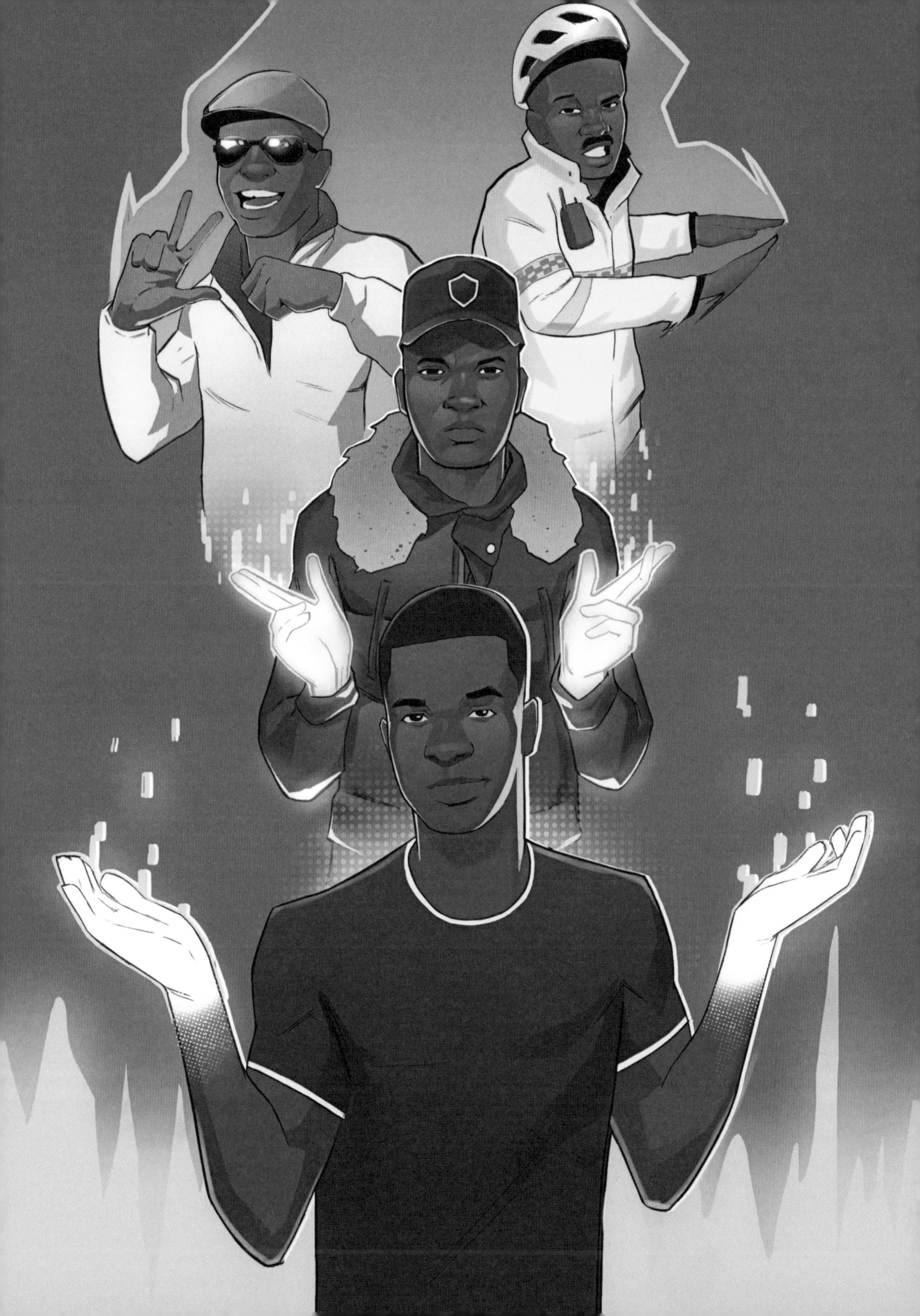

MICHEAL WARD

POWER
Acting

TOOL
Magnetic attraction

Change pose. Freeze. And flash. As the camera lens shutters, the timeline of Micheal Ward snaps together in the sky like magnets, connecting new paths for his face to follow. Micheal has no idea where he is headed, but the magnetic pull is too strong to ignore.

With a heavy attraction to something bigger, the seventeen-year-old model was pulled away from his sixth form, into a performing-arts college that fitted both his aspirations and his education. He kept his symmetrical nose to the sky, following the tug of his future. It led him in front of a camera, modelling. But there was no way that it could stop there. So much more of the world was impatiently waiting to be attached to the young man. From a group of thousands, the Jamaican face and flavour of Micheal caught the attention of JD Sports. His face arrested walls and billboards across the UK. Passers-by would stop and stare, pulled towards the hypnotic eyes that were later to snatch the attention of *Top Boy* and *Blue Story* producers. The character of Jamie in *Top Boy* snapped around the frame of Micheal like a magnet. Jamie took over his walk, his mind and his style. But, even with somebody else wearing his body, the world was still in love with Micheal Ward. On a trip to LA, Busta Rhymes placed his hands on Micheal's shoulders, told him how fond he was of him. The producer of *Blue Story* was also drawn in by the same allure and cast him as Marco.

His exceptional performances not only attracted global billboards, but also a BAFTA award.

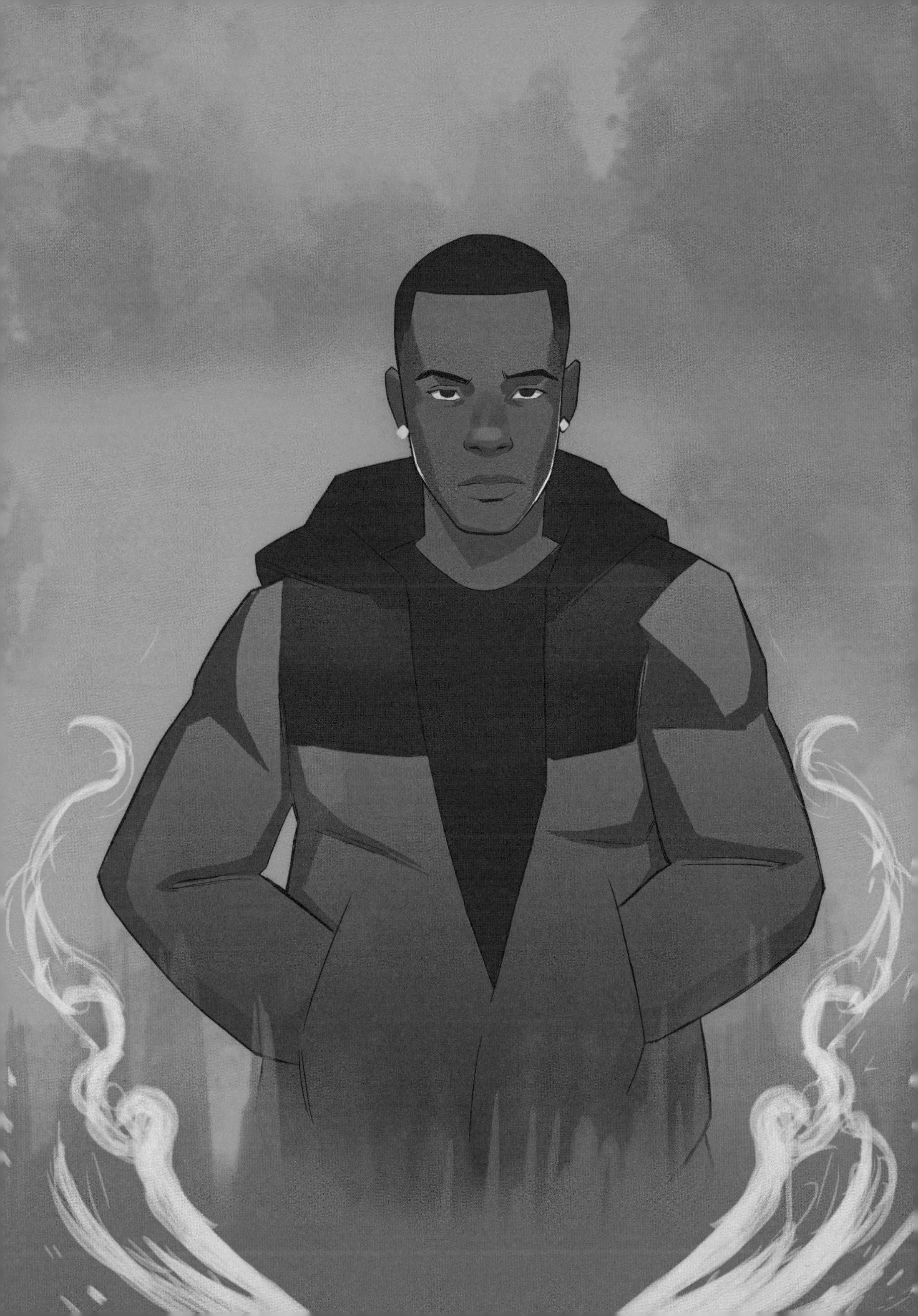

MO GILLIGAN

POWER
Comedy

TOOL
Laughing lens

There lives a well-known belief that every cloud has its silver lining. A lesser-known truth is that everything has a funny streak tucked inside it, waiting to be extracted by a Laughter Master and explode in our bellies. Only a few Masters roam the earth and the most powerful Laughter Master of them all is the 'comedian'.

Mo Gilligan first discovered his amusing ability to see through a laughing lens whilst living a double life. He was labouring in a Levi's shop during the day but transformed into the saviour of strangers' smiles by night at various comedy shows. His laughing lens allowed him to see humour where the ordinary person could not. Gilligan mentally records life and awakens the laughter that sits silently beneath Britain. He then delicately moulds the humour into an arrow to be fired under a spotlight, through his electric smile, deep into the grinning faces of audiences across the world. During his Coupla Cans Tour, the globe vibrated with laughter as he turned the truly serious into the unbearably hilarious, earning his title as Britain's Funniest Man. All London shows sold out in two minutes.

In discovering how to inject humour past the screen and into people's homes, his skits travelled the circuits of the internet to reach the biggest celebrities in the world, from Drake to Anthony Joshua. Not only did Netflix crave a dose of Mo, but Channel 4 gave him *The Lateish Show with Mo Gilligan* to inject the nation with laughs.

Unsurprisingly, people have become obsessed with the man able to welcome them back into their own laughter.

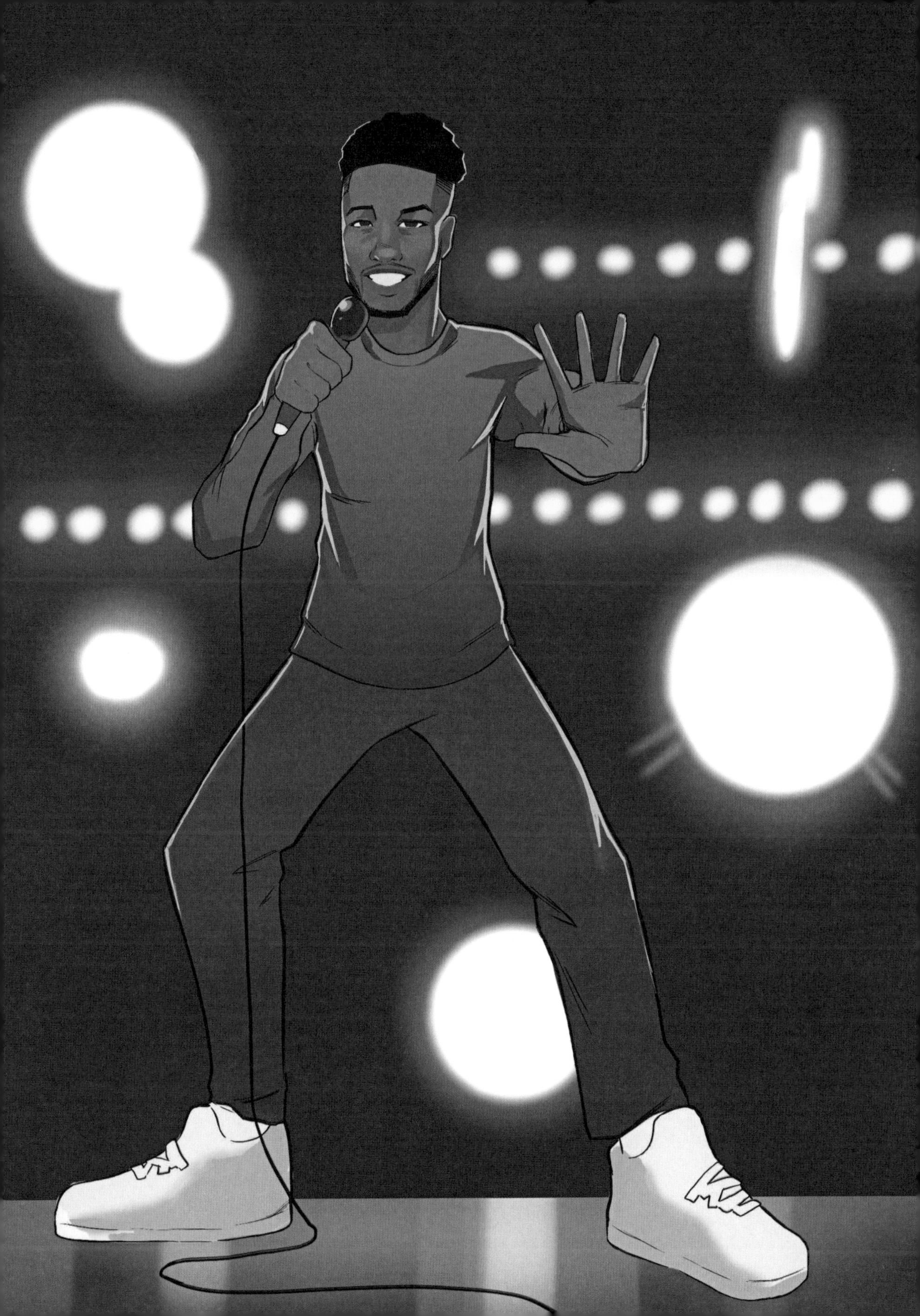

MUSA OKWONGA

POWER
Wielding words

TOOL
His body

Wielders of words remain some of the most important titans in history. Great men such as Musa Okwonga let the world into their bodies to then feed it back to us in a way we can understand. He lets people, things and events twist and turn in his stomach until full sentences are birthed. Sometimes the world wants to be read as a poem, and Okwonga's collection *Eating Roses for Dinner* is a transcript of life's many magical happenings in verse. Sometimes the world needs more people to see it for its imbalance. Musa Okwonga has spent years letting equality marinate in his stomach, weaving journalism together with human rights, migration and colour. His delicate approach to communication was sharpened during his time as Director for Press and Communications at the Institute for Philanthropy in London and New York. Since winning the 1996 WHSmith Young Writers' Competition, Okwonga has pulled words from all industries, including football. He co-wrote and presented the BBC World Service's flagship documentary about the World Cup in Brazil, *The Burden of Beauty.*

The Bible. The Communist Manifesto. The Declaration of Independence. The national anthem. Words have continued to be the most defining weapon in history. They sit on our lips as reminders of who we are. Whether it's the language we speak or the proverbs we remember our parents telling us as kids, words cut through time and pin us to our identity.

Musa's words have pulled him together as a black man living in Berlin, writing poetry, writing on football, writing on communicating and, ultimately, writing us into new ideas.

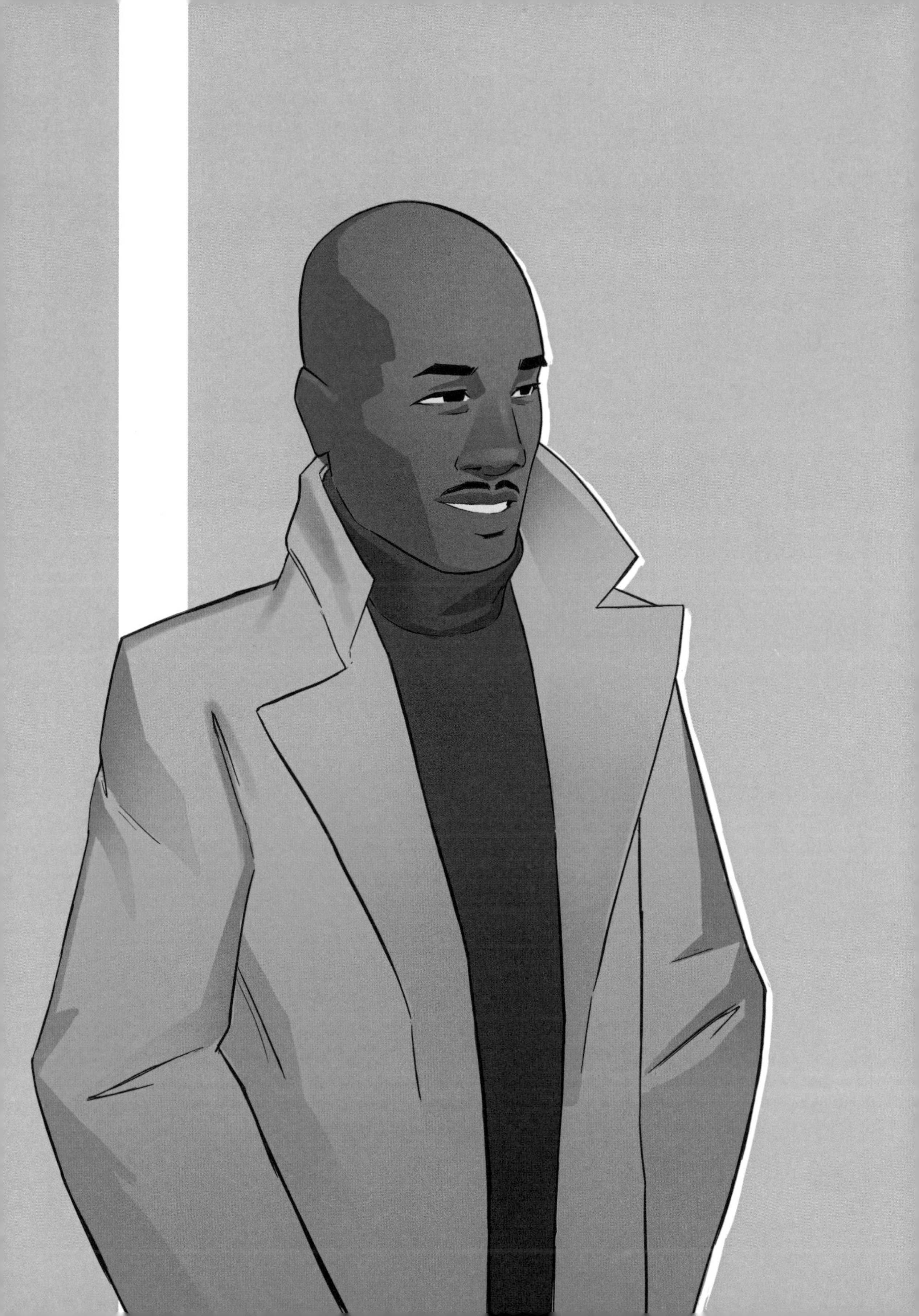

OMARI McQUEEN

POWER
Food

TOOL
Veganism

'I'm sick.' As the words crash out of his mum's lips, they steal the air from Omari McQueen's seven-year-young lungs. For a moment, his world is suspended in darkness and worry suffocates the room. He forces himself to pull another breath, hoping that it will carry something other than fear into his body and stabilise him. As the thick air slices through Omari's trembling lips and cuts through the pulsing lump in his throat, it runs down his frozen body like a force cracking through ice. As the bullet of air nears the rim of his stomach, something extraordinary happens. Dazzling colours begin to beam from his skin. Sparkling carrot-orange and glistening blackberry-blue splashes the walls of his family kitchen.

This is a spectacle that his parents have since got used to seeing whenever Omari begins creating his delicious vegan meals. So delicious that even through his YouTube cooking tutorials, the belly of the world rumbles so passionately, that Omari's homemade dips spill from his kitchen into kitchens across countries. He calls his dips, snacks, seasoning packs and juice packs 'Dipalicious' . . . And the world agrees!

CEO Omari McQueen is the youngest award-winning vegan chef in the UK. But it doesn't stop there. Despite only living in his body for twelve years, he has a remarkable understanding of what each food does and the global benefits of going vegan. Omari won PETA's Compassionate Kids Award for using his entrepreneurial flair to help animals.

The more people eat his exquisite food, the more stomachs begin to glow the delicious and healthy colours of veganism.

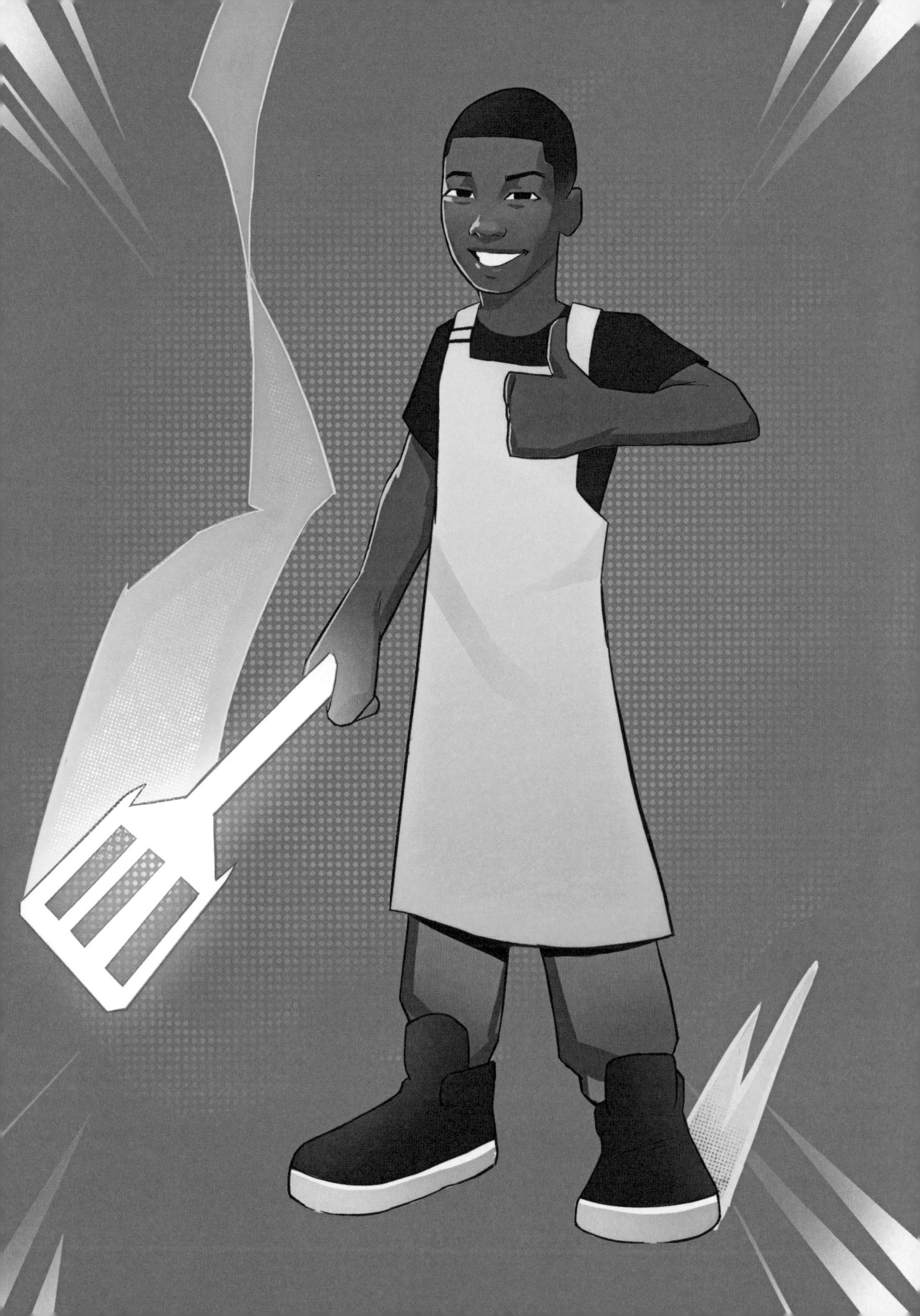

PRINCESS K

POWER
Dance

TOOL
Internal speaker

You could hear a pin drop. Even the wind had silenced its whistle. People's jaws froze mid-sentence and everybody's eyes were drawn to the huge pyramid stage. This was the Glastonbury moment that had been marinating deep in the young bones of Princess K for a decade, the exact amount of time that she had been alive.

As soon as Princess K learnt to walk, she decided that it would be so much more fun to dance through life than stroll through it. Something between her ears owned a speaker, and she danced along to her very own soundtrack. Under the table in school, her feet would tap along to the rhythm that never rested inside of her. Corridors became Princess K's runway and stage to perform on. If anyone was lucky enough to catch her dancing, the same bug would infect them instantly — sweat and smiles breaking from their faces, the music shaking up their hearts. Stormzy wanted the world to dance, and he knew that only Princess K had the power to drop the groove into the 150,000 people watching from the Glastonbury field and the millions online. The entire globe began to wiggle its hips and move its feet when Princess K took to the stage. In a matching tracksuit to Stormzy, she commanded the attention of millions. A glow followed each of her perfectly timed moves, spitting coloured lights in all directions as she danced like a firework in control of its launch. The explosions packed within Princess K have been released on stages across the world with Teni, D'banj and Little Simz.

The world waits impatiently for twelve-year-old Princess K to inject it with her groove...

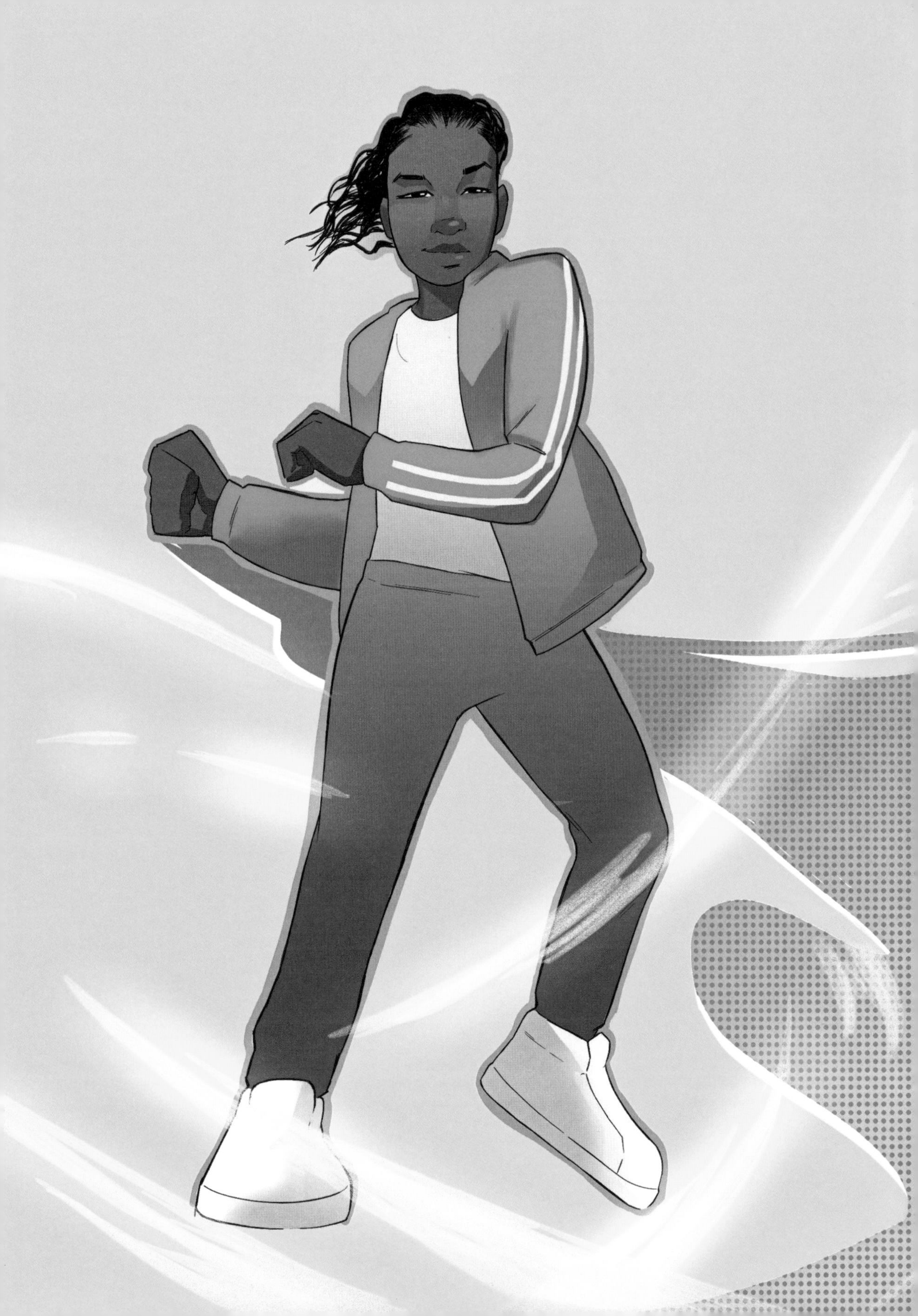

RAPMAN

POWER	**TOOL**
Writing	Seeds of life

Growing up in Deptford planted the first seed into the mighty mouth and mind of Andrew Onwubolu. As the years performed before him, the seed was sprouting into a soundtrack to his life. There was a melody to the madness that occurred in his area, and a beat for the heart of each of his boys. He watered the seed until it grew into the musical three-part YouTube drama *Shiro's Story*. Onwubolu locked himself in with the seeds of all he had actually lived through, and sat whilst they sprouted around his mind, creating rhyming couplets, songs and melodies that would eventually bloom through the mouth of Rapman: an authentic narrator, telling the stories of our time in a raw, artistic and honest way. The streets finally had a real mirror talking back to them in the language that they spoke. It hit the hearts of over ten million people online, and soon enough, the wider film world recognised the power within the growing forest. Real recognised real, and Jay-Z had to sign him to his label, Roc Nation, stretching those seeds into an entire jungle through the cinema hit *Blue Story*. Andrew let his mind grow into new areas to ensure that the casting, costumes, script and directing of the film was as he saw it growing up. The power within the rawness challenged the oppressive side of society who attempted to deforest the film during its first week.

But what's real and what's rap will always come to light, and the film went on to make £4.5 million despite the cinema ban.

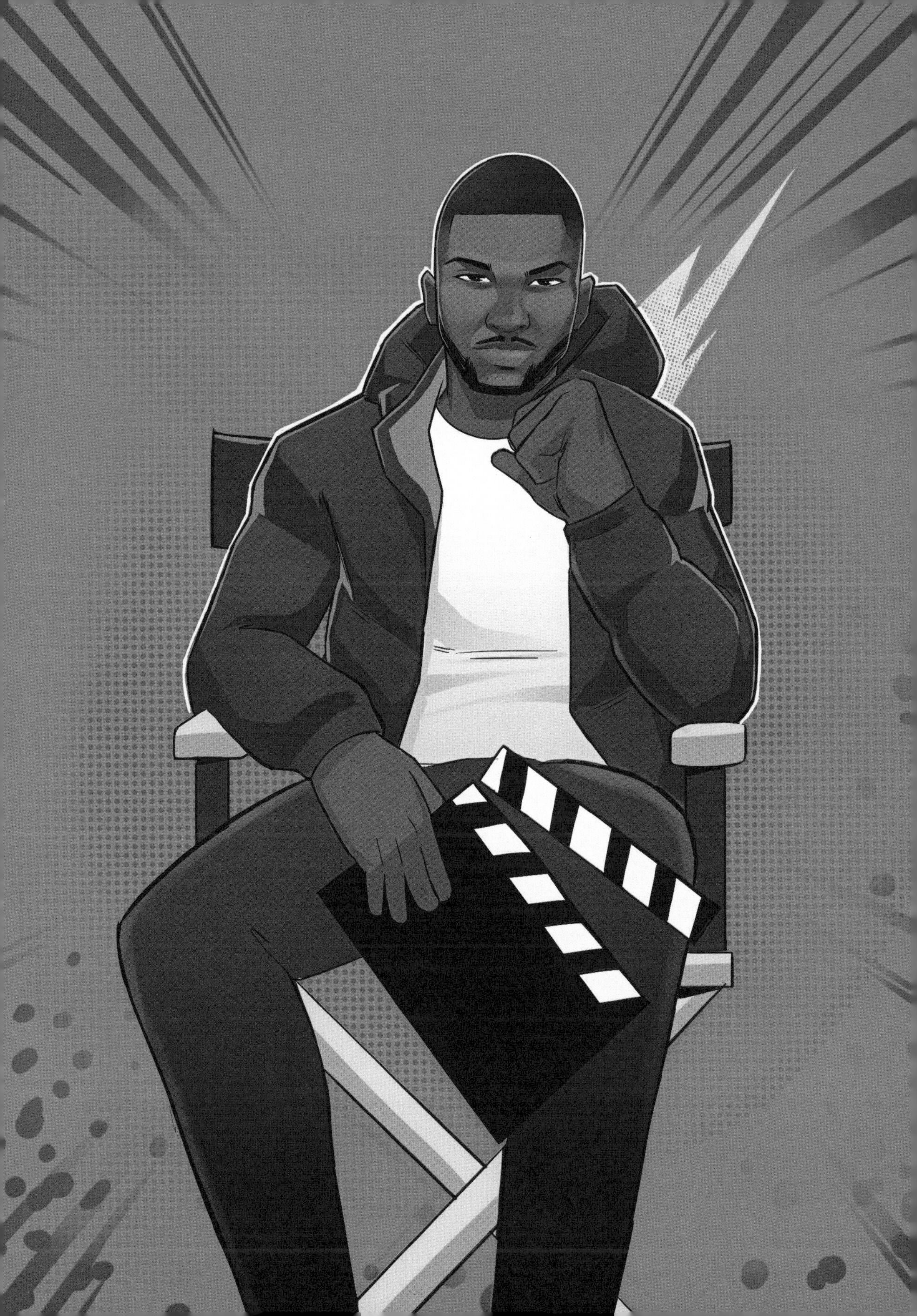

REGGIE YATES

POWER
Storytelling

TOOL
Television

It was love at first sight. Or perhaps trust at first sight. At eight years old, when Reggie Yates stepped onto the set of *Desmond's*, an arrow of light beamed from the cameras, crossing the studio and spinning around Reggie's willing heart. Sparks pierced through his skin and into the eyes of the directors who did not fully know how powerful this new connection was about to become. Nobody did, not even Reggie. All he knew was that he had become joined to television in a way that others around him didn't seem to be.

As the years went on, various television channels activated different connections in him over and over again. From *Top of the Pops* and *Doctor Who* to the MOBO awards, as a presenter, actor and voice-over artist. The bond between the two was so complex and delicate, that when the time came to document the more controversial and emotional stories of the world, television could only trust its soulmate Reggie Yates. He protected this union by promising only honest and integrity-filled storytelling. Taking the relationship between himself, television and the viewers very seriously, he spent time behind bars in Texas, and joined Unit 27 of the 56th Infantry Battalion in Acapulco to live and document the life of an ordinary soldier fighting on the front line of a war against Mexico's powerful cartels. He continues educating the world with documentaries such as *Teen Gangs*, *Criminal Britain*, *Extreme Russia* and *Extreme South Africa*. As the connection between the two matures, Reggie has learnt to express it in loads of spaces. He has written, produced and directed award-winning short films and the feature film *Pirates* that is itching to find its home on cinema screens.

Reggie Yates constantly lends his whole self to the service of storytelling. Writing, acting and directing, he shows the world what stories can become in safe hands.

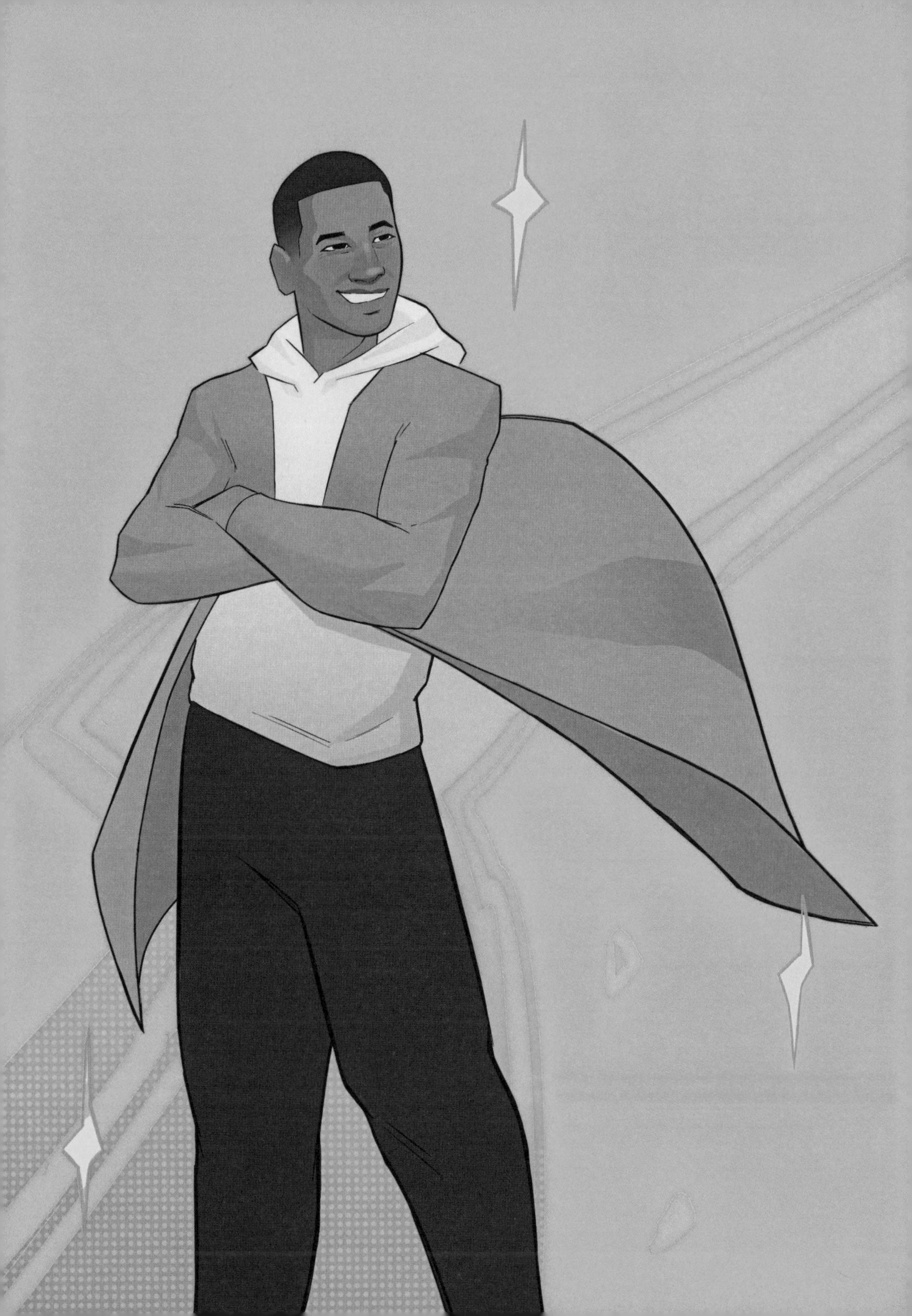

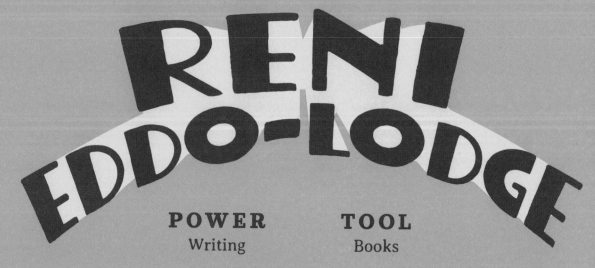

RENI EDDO-LODGE

POWER
Writing

TOOL
Books

The average person freezes in the face of trouble. But not Reni Eddo-Lodge. At nineteen, when the portals of feminism and university introduced her to the details of an unjust world, a ripple of rage tore its way up her body to crowd her arm, and her fist caught fire for the first time.

After some time, the fire spat from the tips of her fingers into various newspaper articles. *The New York Times*, the *Guardian*, *Dazed* and *Vice* all bowed their heads as Reni Eddo-Lodge uprooted inaccurate and dated ideas. But the papers were not enough. An article could not encompass the injustices that had filled the lives of black people for centuries. There was more to be said. So Reni thrust her Nigerian-British fist into an air of blackness under a white-dominated sky, and let history happen to her body. With a fist raised, she opened her entire self: not just her writing arm, but a podcasting mouth too. A jaw-dropping book and podcast were launched from her skin.

Why I'm No Longer Talking to White People About Race is not just a book: it is the shared frustration of black people everywhere — and the undeniable reasons for it. It is no wonder that the book has gone on to win the Jhalak Prize and many more. Eddo-Lodge became the first black British author to top the UK book chart; *Why I'm No Longer Talking to White People About Race* became a *New York Times* bestseller, and from it came an equally powerful podcast, *About Race*, that has won Eddo-Lodge three Lovie awards.

In Reni Eddo-Lodge, the force of black fists found a voice on the page.

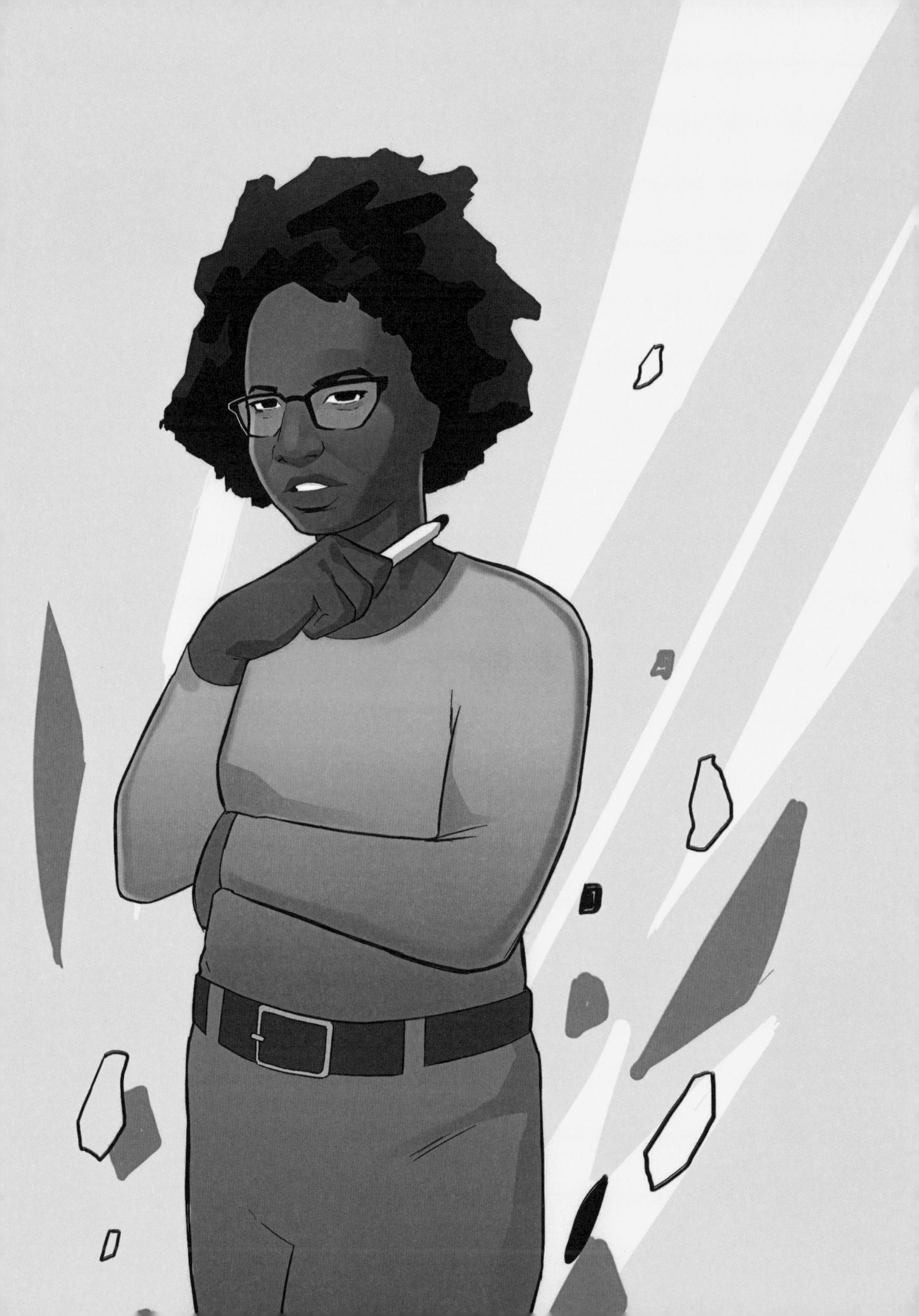

POWER
Code-switching

TOOL
Acting

Riz Ahmed grew up as a British Pakistani. That meant his world was often split into smaller worlds that wanted different versions of him. One needed him to wear a salwar kameez and speak Urdu. The other needed him in a suit speaking English. At first, living in between the two worlds confused him, but slowly he began to realise how powerful it was to bring the different sides of his character together, showing the world how beautiful a more colourful picture can be. He wanted to show the world that inside each of us there is all of us.

Riz decided he would use his superpower to tell this truth in as many ways as possible. Harnessing the power of code-switching, he found himself putting on various capes in film, politics and even music!

Carlton Drake wanted to rescue humanity in the blockbuster film *Venom*. Bodhi Rook needed to destroy the Death Star in *Rogue One: A Star Wars Story*. The Hamilton Mixtape wanted to expose the truth of who built American society (and were never thanked for it) in the song 'Immigrants'. Riz was able to play all these roles, and become all these people.

Although the outside of Riz remains fluid, able to shine and flow into a different character, sound or industry whenever he desires, on the inside Riz's powers are always focused on the same thing — to try and stretch our culture to a point where everyone feels they belong in it, and they don't have to code-switch at all.

Whether in Hollywood, the House of Commons or the Billboard chart, Ahmed's heart pumps out the same message — there is no 'Us and Them', just Us.

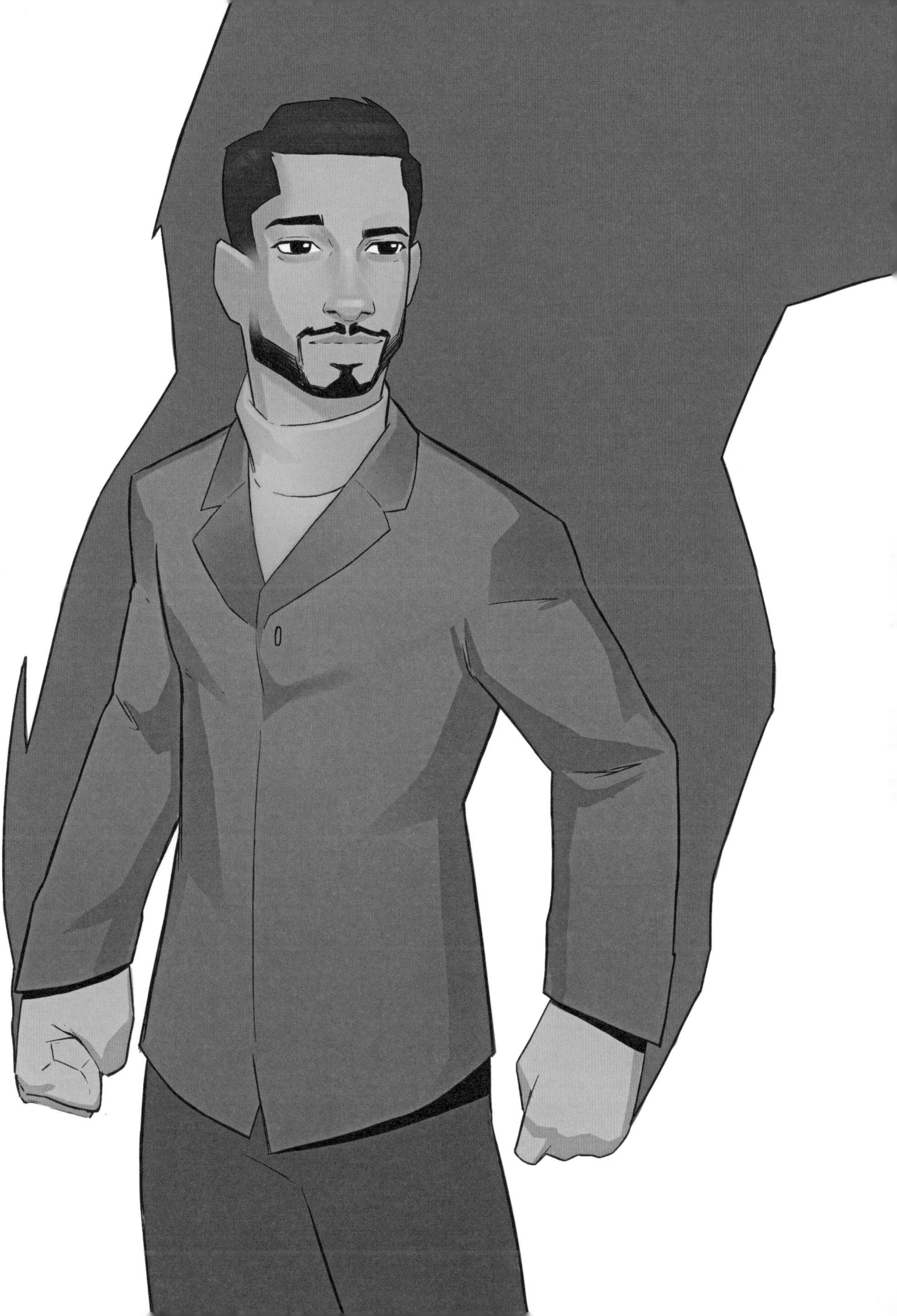

TANYA COMPAS

POWER
Pulling the voice
from the voiceless

TOOL
Ears

It sat on the floor of their stomachs, cross-legged with society's fingers clipping their lips together. There, the voice of the youth waited to one day feel brave and bold enough to climb up the rungs of their ribs, swirl in the waters of their heavy hearts and pull that weight up through their mouths to finally give their lips the truth that they had been waiting for. Tanya Compas cast a gentle fishing rod into the bodies of teens everywhere, and pulled back the duvet of silence that had stapled so many young black people's tongues down to the floor with their fear. And she told them to speak. To allow themselves the grace to work out what their bodies were trying to say to them, but out loud and with the support of peers and Tanya's ears.

Tanya in many ways acts as a compass, directing the youth into communities and opportunities that will encourage and inspire them to be confident. With her cape as a youth worker tied proudly around her shoulders, she creates a world where kids who have never seen themselves on television or in magazines can follow in her footsteps to be in *Vogue*, in newspapers and, most importantly, in love with themselves and their truth. Even when the truth is confusing.

When the truth is anxiety or depression, or when it's self-doubt or denial, Tanya Compas reminds the youth that the truth doesn't need to be perfect — it just needs to be honest.

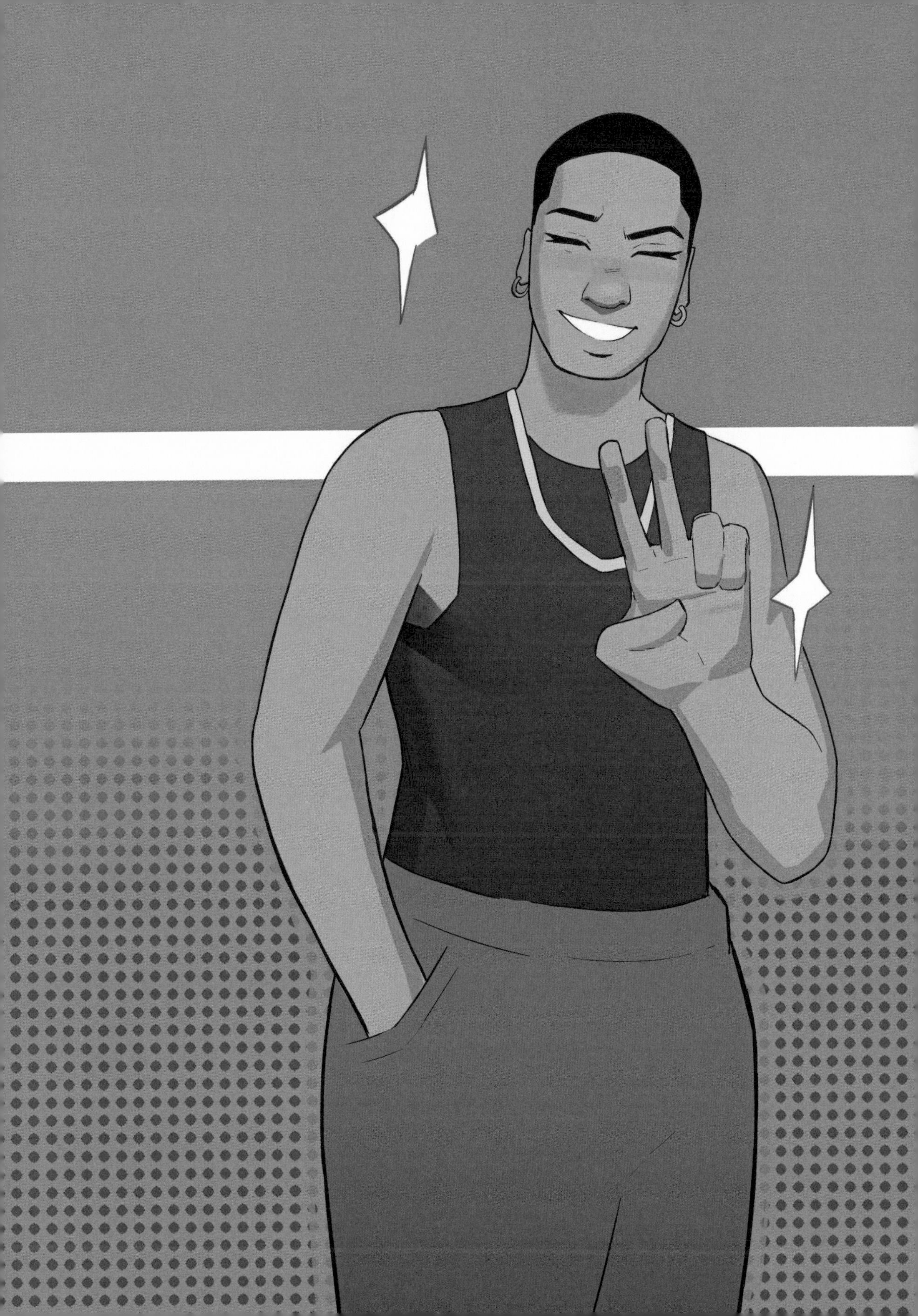

TEMI FAGBENLE

POWER
Basketball

TOOL
Bloodline

One by one, remarkable powers would reveal themselves in each of the twelve Nigerian Fagbenle children — some behind a camera, some inside a textbook, some on the screen and a few on the basketball court. But for Tèmítọpẹ Títílọlá Olúwatóbilọba Fágbénlé, greatness followed her wherever she went — on the WNBA and Olympic basketball courts, at Harvard University and even behind a camera. She carries her power into each of her passions and then overachieves in a major way. Something in her blood in particular glows a more electric shade of crimson. Her entire body becomes a vessel for excellence. Although as an early teen, she was hoping to be the next Serena Williams, being one of twelve super-children meant that her father, Tunde, had to find a way to activate their powers in an affordable way. One day, after tennis practice, a drop of destiny landed in his mind. He finally saw her height for all that it could be, and from that point on, the 6'4" superstar ran straight into the arms of basketball supremacy. At fifteen, less than two years after taking up the sport, she won a full scholarship to Blair Academy in New Jersey, that Luol Deng had also attended. In true perfection of her power, she led Blair to a state title, and was named in the All-American team before over sixty colleges began begging for a piece of her power. Although Temi decided that Harvard was the best place to nurture her talents, she thrives on any court she carries herself on. She has won a championship with every pro team she has been with, including the 2021 Italian Serie A Championship.

Temi Fagbenle's power swims under her skin like a shapeshifting magnet, pulling eyes everywhere — from the Minnesota Lynx to the modelling world.

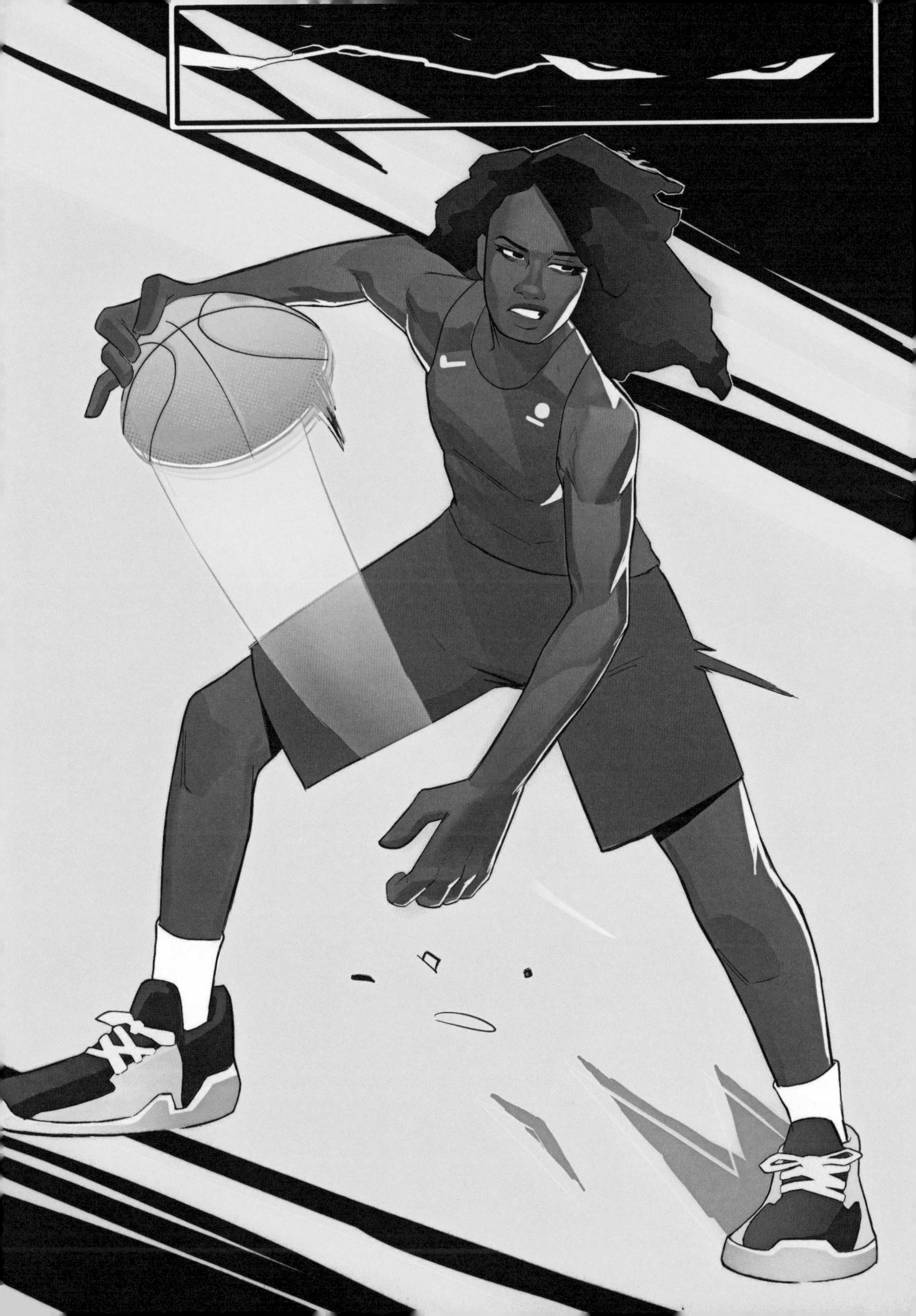

TEMI MWALE

POWER
Justice

TOOL
Knowledge

Some people are moved to tears by injustice. Others are born to live fighting it. Temi Mwale is both. Temi grew up in Grahame Park and from a young age was exposed to how frightening bad leadership can be. As her heart broke over the murder of her good friend Marvin, it opened to be filled with the truth of why so many young people like him were being murdered. The need for justice erupted like a tsunami within her teenage body, channelling all her sadness and swallowing her youthful innocence. The storm continued to rage as she learnt more and more about how racism is the root of so much suffering. Temi Mwale needed to save her city. The yearning triggered a deep study into how a lack of support, education and resources can lead young men to kill, and turn whole populations into victims. As the city got worse, Temi developed her strongest weapon: knowledge. She studied the law, the streets, the system, the politicians, the culture and the youth to finally put on her first cape of many colours: The 4Front Project.

Temi Mwale uncovers the suppressed power within communities — stripping away layers of racism, injustice and discrimination to give power back to the people. She takes the city's broken hearts and her revolutionary mind into rooms with world leaders such as Obama, to convince them to do the right thing.

The groundbreaking force of her compassion, endless strength in her softness and the power she has pulled from heartbreak have immortalised countless young men who have been killed.

They live on through her fiery dedication to their justice.

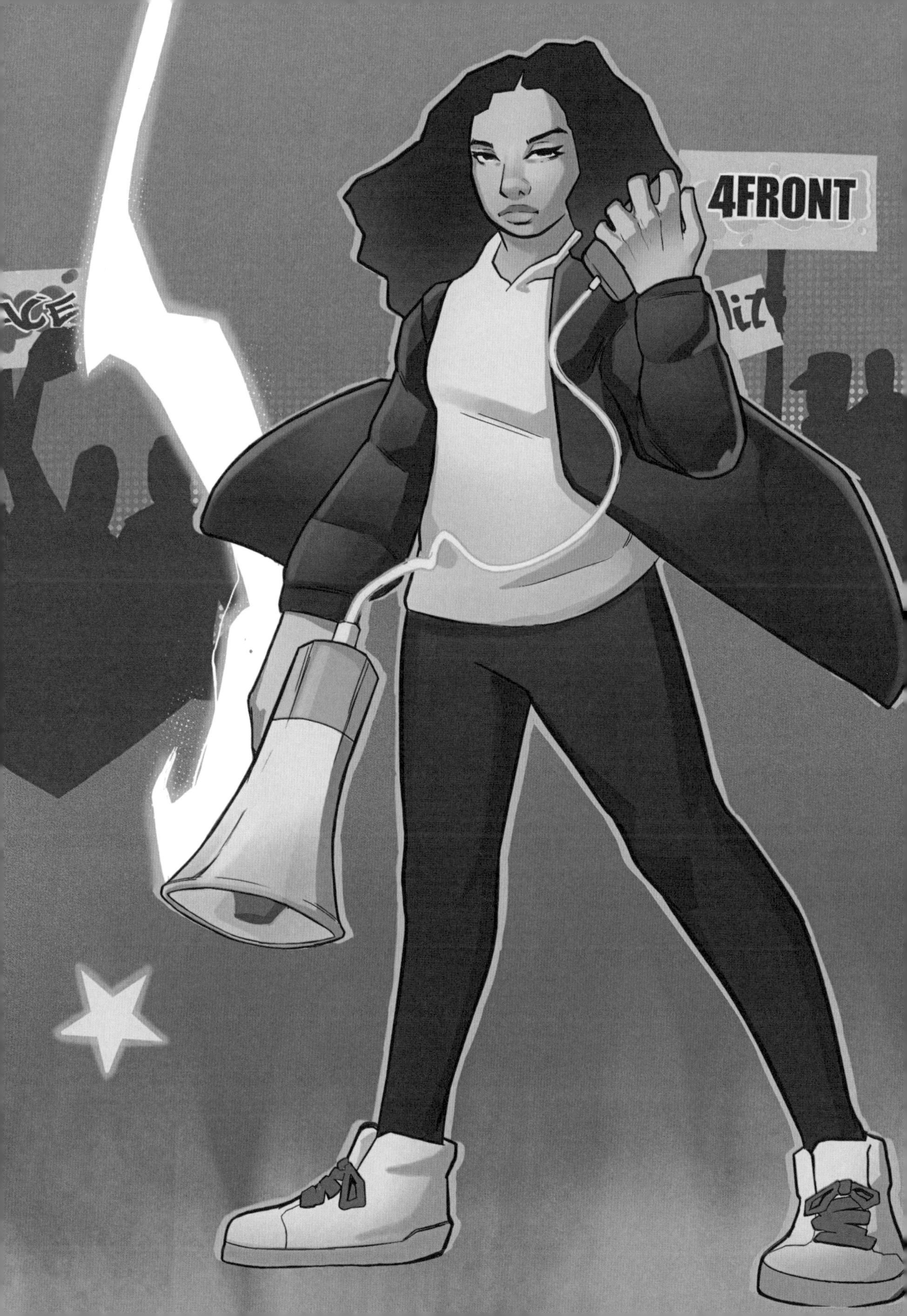
4FRONT

THE KANNEH-MASONS

POWER
Music

TOOL
The heart

The Incredibles use speed and strength. The Avengers use force and might. The Kanneh-Masons use music — a gift from God dropped into the seven seeds that make these remarkable siblings. Each is uniquely gifted in the language of sound and deeply adored by the Royal Academy of Music. The ease with which they give a voice to an instrument stuns the world time and time again as they speak so beautifully and powerfully without opening their lips. The four 'yeses' from the judges of *Britain's Got Talent* were not the only signs of admiration the siblings have enjoyed. They silenced the Royal Variety audience. Sheku Kanneh-Mason let his cello sing at the Duke and Duchess of Sussex's wedding as he showed the world that love is stronger than difference once difference makes space for love. A message that the mother of these super siblings stands with. After Sheku won BBC Young Musician in 2016, she said that she had always been determined 'never to remark on the lack of black people in classical music to her children'. All she needed them to do was believe and do it. And that they did. Eleven-year-old Aminata DID get her grade eight distinction on violin and now has a grade eight on piano. At nine years old, Jeneba DID achieve a grade eight distinction on the piano. Konya DID play for the royal family twice. Isata DID debut at the top of the UK Official Classical Artist Chart, and Braimah DID play the violin with Clean Bandit.

Whilst we breathe and speak with our lips, these siblings learn how music speaks with its own mouth.

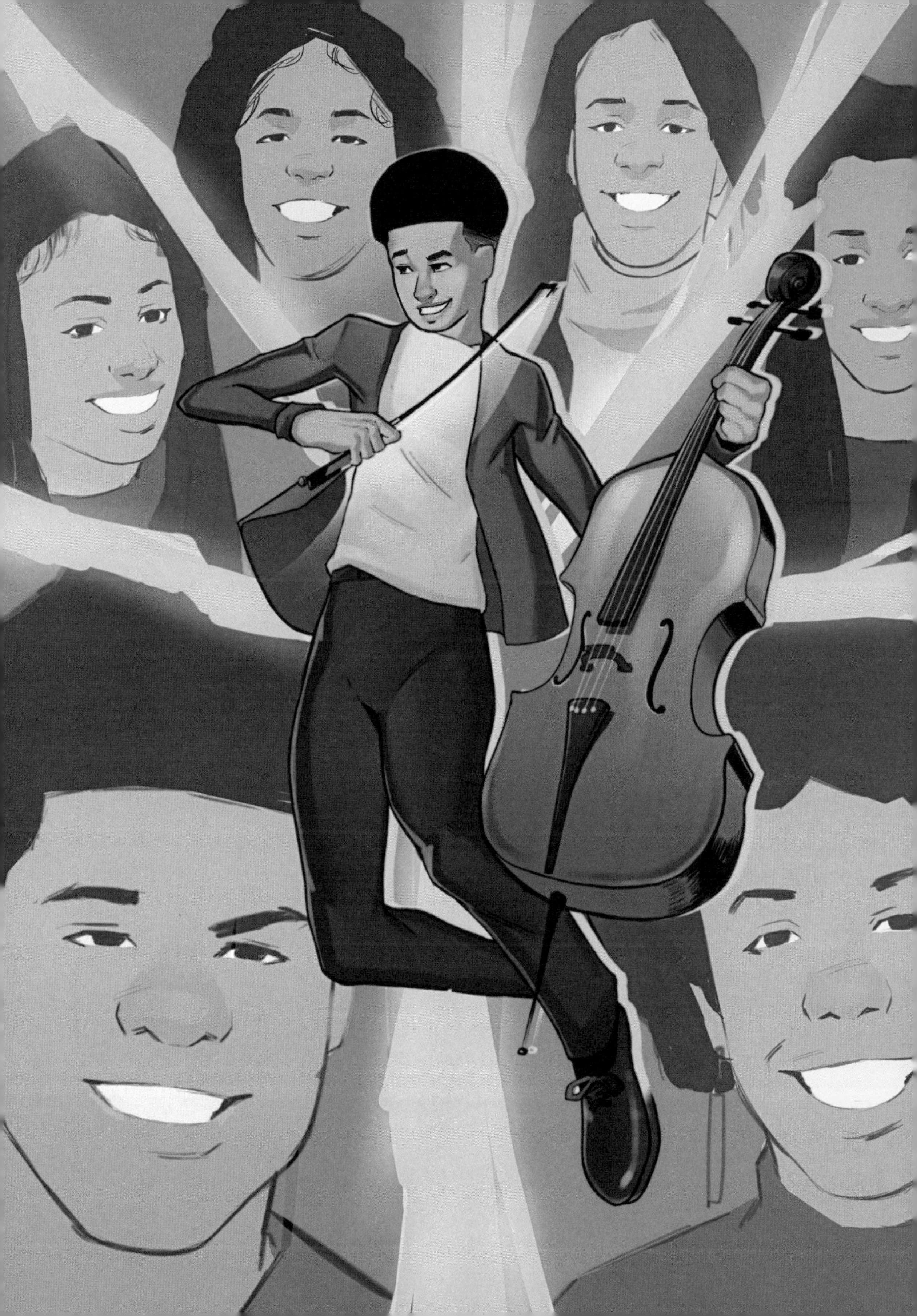

THERESA IKOKO

POWER
Storytelling

TOOL
Knocking

Tap tap tap. She focused on the object in front of her. Tap tap tap. She squeezed her eyes shut. Tap. She turned to each of her eight siblings to see if maybe they could hear it too. But Theresa Ikoko knew it was coming from inside her head. The tapping had been happening for a few years, but recently it seemed to be getting louder and louder. It was as if the more life she experienced and the more time she spent with her family going through love, laughter and loss, the more frequent the tapping and knocking became. It was really distracting during Theresa's time at the University of Oxford where she was studying for a master's degree in criminology. And her brain was overwhelmed by this sense of knocking as she spent time in prisons, leading artistic workshops. It was as if the stories of the rich-but-overlooked lives of those who she met and studied twisted through her ears to land in her brain. But, whilst working in prisons, she began to listen to the knocking instead of fighting it. She let the stories filter onto her laptop. The more she wrote, the lighter the knocking became. One day, she rang her friend and read him one of the plays she had written and, amazed, he forced her to show somebody. The door of her brain had been opened and out poured the award-winning play *Girls*, followed later by her co-written and BAFTA-winning film *Rocks*. Once the door had been opened by producers and agents who loved how familiar the stories felt, the knocking became softer. Now the overlooked characters in Theresa's life do not need to knock so hard to get her attention.

The door has been removed from its hinges and she walks the stories out onto the stage.

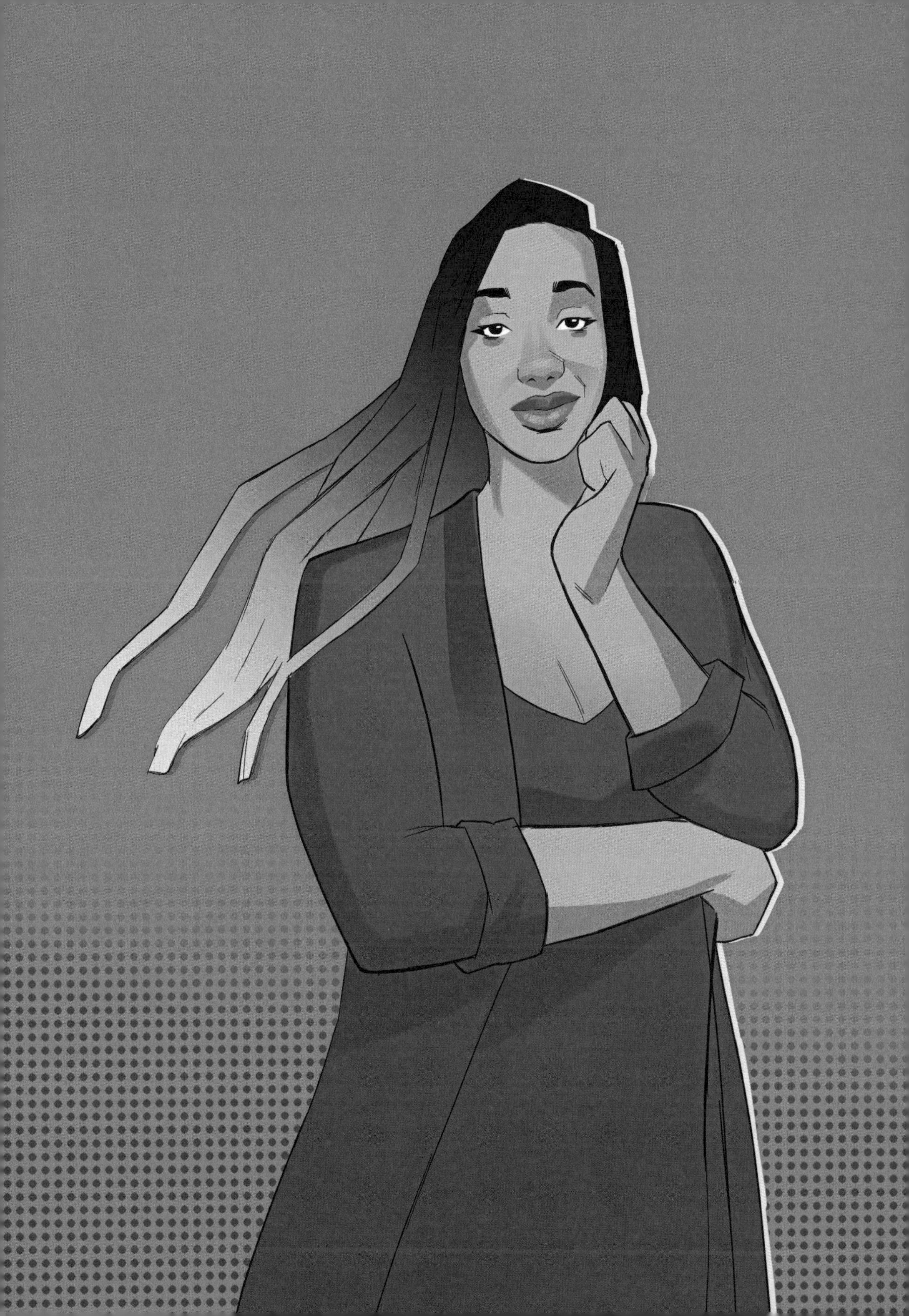

THE TRIPLE CRIPPLES

POWER	TOOL
Disability	3 oppressors

Triple means three. But three does not refer to the number of women that make up The Triple Cripples. Three is the layer cake of oppression that Jumoke Abdullahi and Kym Oliver eat daily. For breakfast, they are fed their skin colour on a plate of racism. For lunch, they eat their gender, and for dinner they finish with a plate of disability.

Jumoke and Kym are filled to the brim with the disadvantage of living in a world that doesn't always acknowledge them. But these ladies are not just trying to be seen. Through YouTube and blogging, they are telling the world why they should be celebrated. They don't swallow and wallow in the face of difficulty, they smile and wave. Something in their wiring doesn't allow them to remain silent and invisible. As each corner of the oppressive triangle digests inside them, it goes through a vigorous reconstruction in their bellies. Oppression is burnt to liquid and then re-moulded into empowerment, and their disadvantages are flipped on their heads to resurface as very important topics of conversation. Usually, the heaviness of a triple attack can weigh lips together, but the science is reversed when it comes to The Triple Cripples. And they are adamant about sharing their power with other disadvantaged groups, whilst also breaking the stereotypes that surround them. They wear the name 'Cripple' like a medal of honour. They take it to the BBC, the *Metro* and *Black Ballad,* and bring a new meaning to the once offensive term. The Triple Cripples, with Polio and Multiple Sclerosis between them, are deeper than their disability, more remarkable than their race and far greater than their gender because they get to wear all three suits at the same time.

The power of confidence unstoppable. X3.

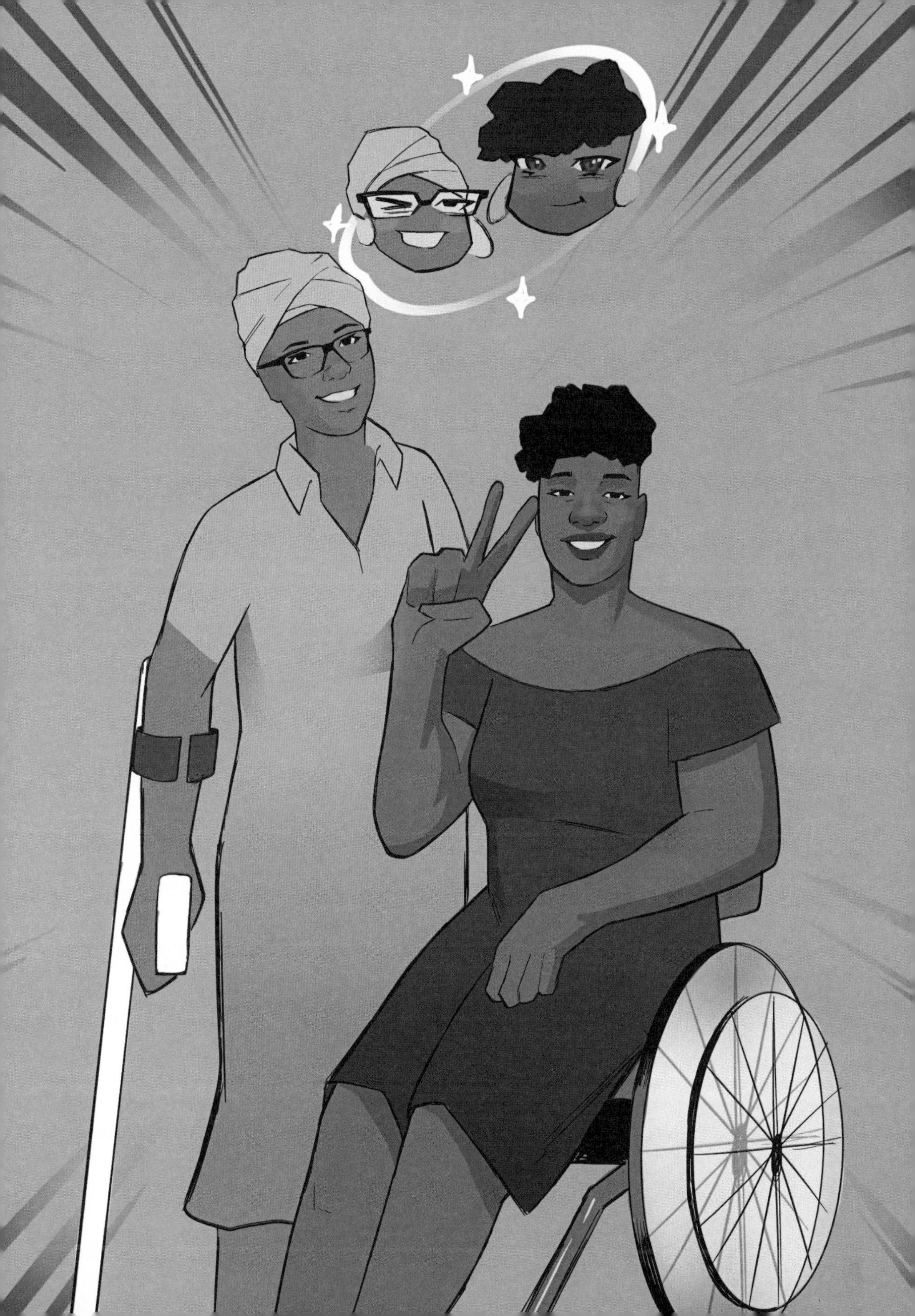

WILLIAM ADOASI

POWER
Changing lives

TOOL
Watches

The ticking is so close William Adoasi isn't sure whether it is coming from his wrist or inside his head. In an attempt to suspend time and focus, he squeezes his eyes shut and, within a second of his eyelids crashing into each other, the world cuts loose and spirals out of control. As he struggles to stabilise his brain, the ticking gets louder and louder, demanding all of the space between his ears. Just as William is about to claw his eyes back open, the world around him comes to a standstill. The clock strikes midnight, and his eyes snap open to face the Vitae watch on his wrist. The glowing gold rim becomes the mouth of a well, holding hundreds of moving images in its grip. As William Adoasi stares deeper and deeper at the watch face, images begin to fall into focus. He sees the beaming smile of a child he and his wife had met in South Africa. He watches joy rebound from the child's feet as he skips to school in his new school uniform. The uniform that is able to be bought for a child who needs it, following the sale of each watch. Utterly overwhelmed, William forces himself to look deeper into the watch face and catches a glimpse of the child's future. He watches him graduate and become a doctor who goes on to own a practice that serves his community for free. Eyes wet, he pulls away from the watch. But this time more confident in his vision to grow a fashion brand that saves lives. As he steps into his meetings with Richard Branson and other key players in the worlds of business and the arts, his pitch is made simple. He puts a watch on their wrist and invites them into the legacy of each child whose life will be transformed through the purchase.

Vitae means 'lives' in Latin and William Adoasi is committed to transforming as many as possible.

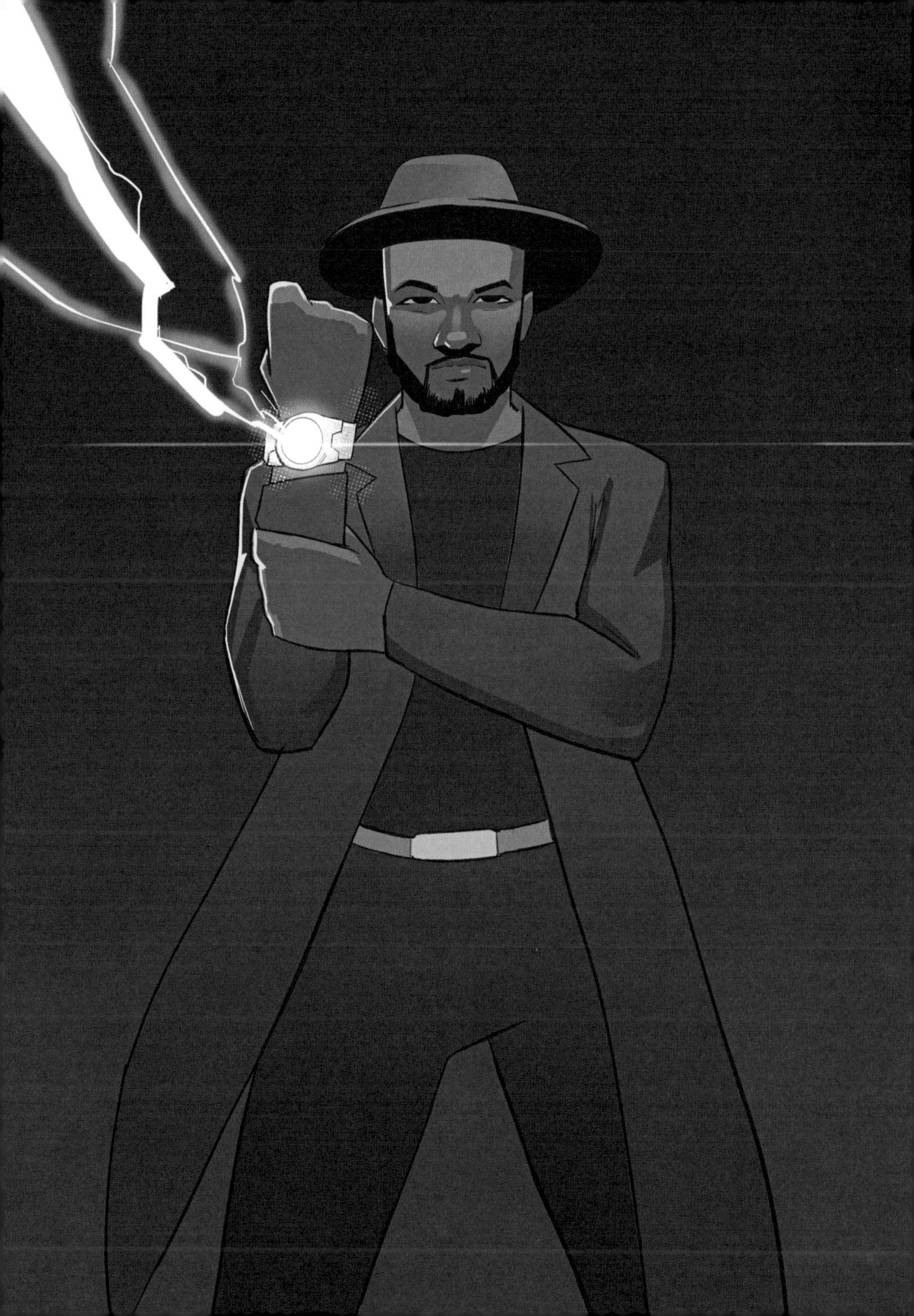

YINKA ILORI

POWER
Design

TOOL
Palms

It sizzled under his skin like a firework, waiting to shatter the sky into coins of colour. Deep beneath Yinka Ilori's British accent sat a light-green tongue, pulsing at the chance to somehow release the Nigerian stories and parables that he'd grown up on. Despite being raised in London, the infectious sounds, smells and style of West Africa had seduced each of his senses. All of them, that is, except sight. His limbs may lift and dance themselves into a festival once they hear Afrobeats, and his mouth may celebrate as the flavours of Jollof and Suya journey passed his lips, but growing up in a grey London after leaving his family home, left his eyes asleep with no energetic colours to wake them and inspire them to look for more. Yinka Ilori needed to pick up as much of London as possible between his playful palms and squeeze the colour back into people's lives. He lifted the troubled-looking tunnel from Battersea, tilted it into the River Thames and splashed a carnival of colour across the concrete. When tasked with making a new installation for the grounds of the Dulwich Picture Gallery, he knew he needed to walk his hands back to the streets of Lagos. He sat in his studio and allowed the textures, shapes and sounds of Africa to soak into him. Once his palms were charged, they pulled in wood, wax, shine, noise and shapes to create the sight-stealing, smile-inducing 'Colour Palace'.

Yinka Ilori continues to study design and furniture to understand how he can inject the landscape of the world with the festival of colour that stains every part of his body.

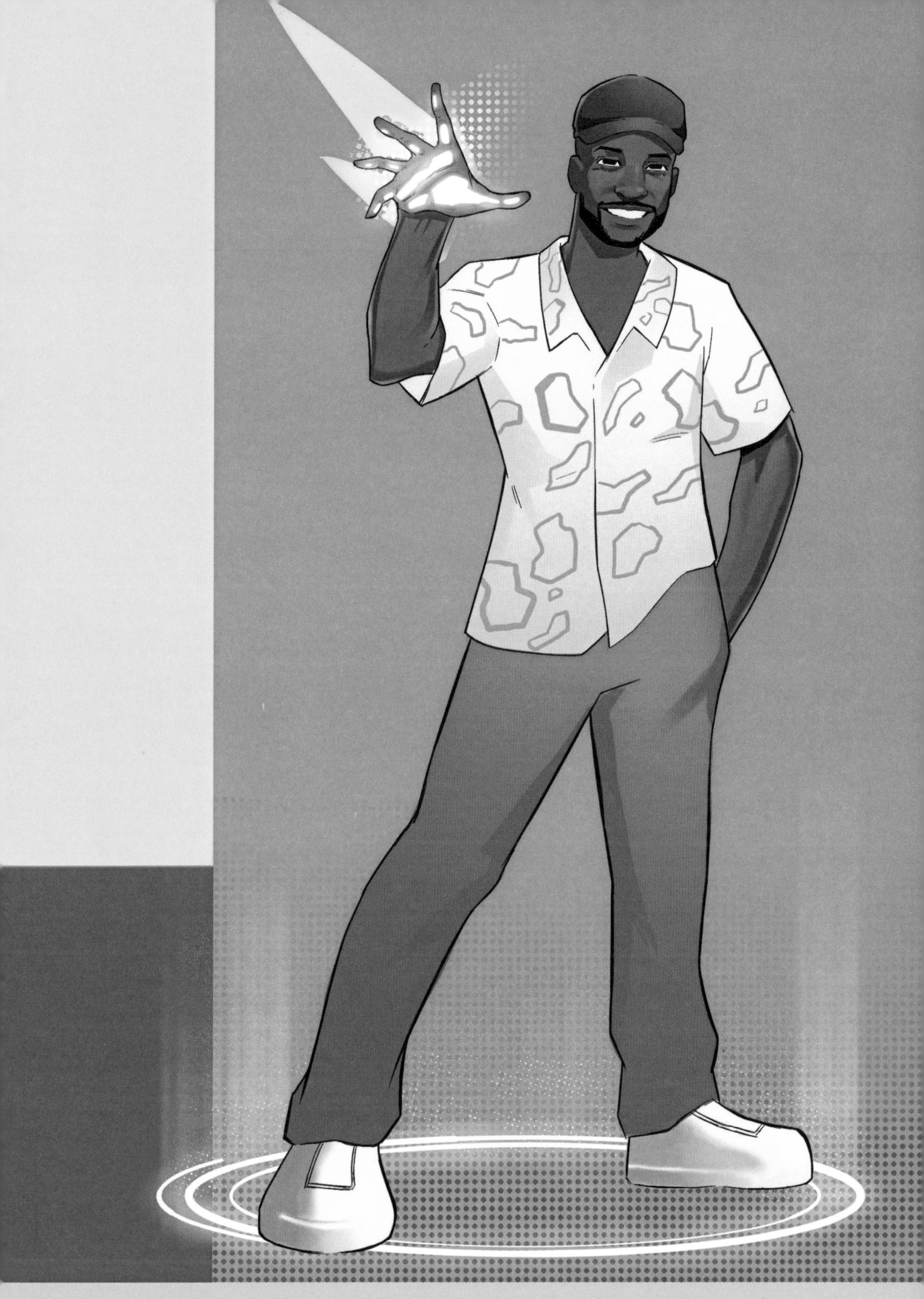

DRAW YOUR OWN SUPERHERO

WRITE YOUR OWN SUPERHERO

....

....

....

....

....

....

....

....

....

....

....

....

SOPHIA THAKUR

You can find Sophia Thakur's powerful but tender poetry on the Ted Talk stage, in *Vogue*, on popular musicians' albums, in school curriculums worldwide, in campaigns for Calvin Klein and Unilever. Her mesmerising performances and messages on love, loss, race, equality, family and empowerment have flown her across the world onto hundreds of stages, moving thousands at a time to tears. Sophia Thakur is the gentle rhyming voice of her generation. She has been invited to perform at over 100 universities and schools, for royal families, politicians and various celebrities, who can't help but fall under her spell as she re-introduces people to poetry in a completely new way.

Her poetic commentary on the world around us encourages listeners and readers to think about their true feelings. To work out why they feel the way they do, or why other people feel the way that they do. With empathy at the centre of her work, Sophia Thakur tells other people's stories on stage, in hope of bridging the gap between different walks of life.

At school Sophia only ever saw black people in history textbooks, in chains. Writing this book was important to her, to give young kids something to be proud of and aspire to.

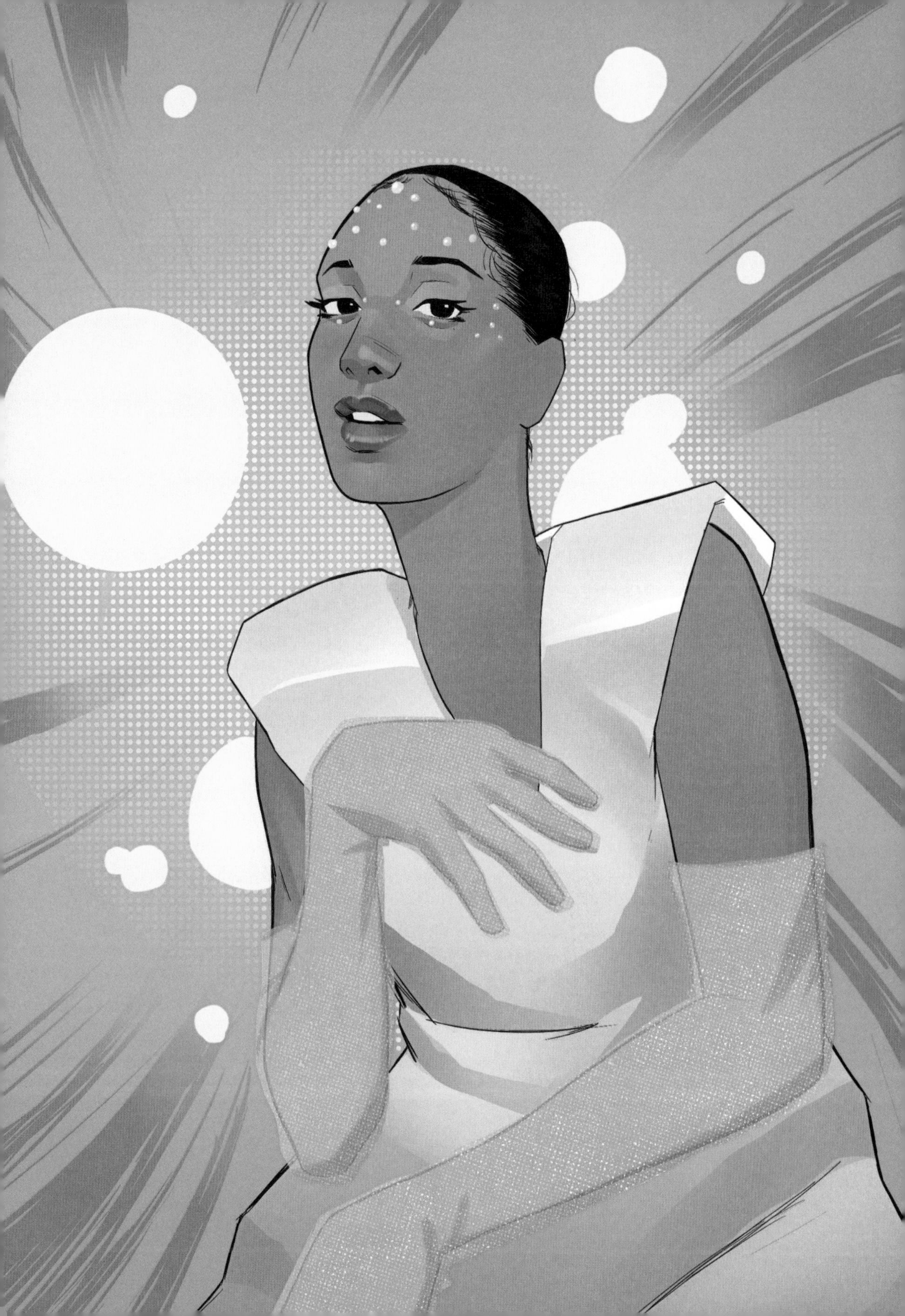

DENZELL DANKWAH

My name is Denzell Dankwah and I'm a 21-year-old British-born Ghanaian. When I was around the age of five my parents and I moved from Croydon to Northampton where my sisters and I grew up. I'm currently in my final year at the University of Gloucestershire studying Illustration (BA Hons). Comic books and graphic novels influence my art heavily and it is my love for the medium that encouraged me to start drawing at an early age. I was always creative throughout school and tried to find any excuse to draw: from doodling in notebooks to drawing pictures for my friends during lunchtime. It's always been something I've enjoyed doing, so having the opportunity to portray such huge figures and role models as heroes for young readers to look up to has been an amazing experience.

I was around six years old when I got my first batch of comic books — I remember one of them being an *X-Men* comic. I would just look at the illustrations, sometimes not even reading what was happening. I was amazed how artists could create such cool pages, so much so that I would try and draw the same thing. My parents were always supportive and they would get art books for me to learn from. Illustrating a book is something I've always pursued but didn't think would happen this soon. For that I'm grateful to the incredible team at #Merky Books, for giving me a chance to do what I love.

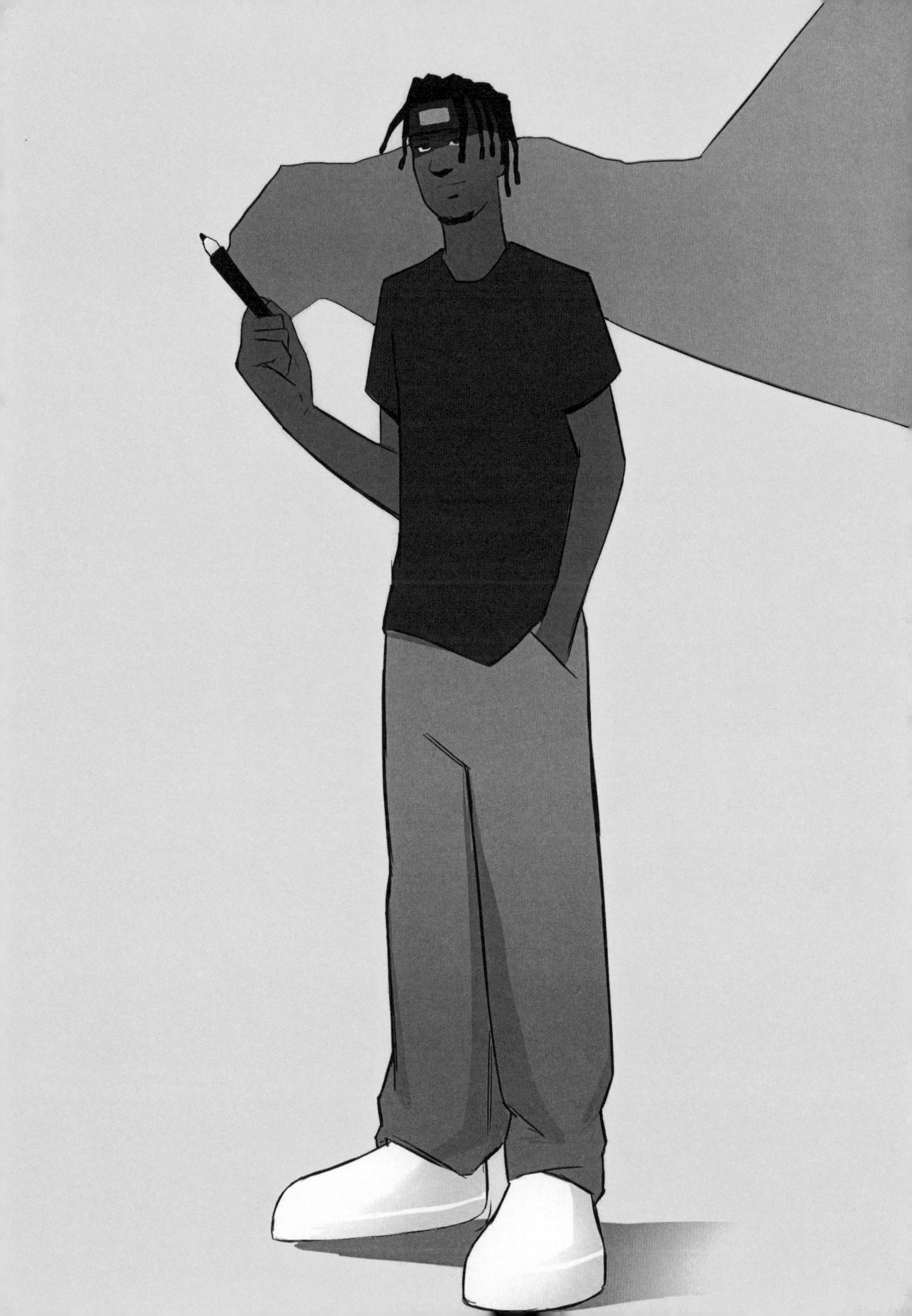

ACKNOWLEDGEMENTS

I'm so sure that it is love that turns a person
into a powerful hero. The first superheroes
I ever met were my odds-defying parents.
A father who never gave my brothers and
me room to ever feel unprotected. A mum
whose service to us was our first example
of God. As a child, I wouldn't have put
them in the category of 'human'. They were
legends, undeniable and unstoppable. How
blessed I am to grow to see them today, for
what they truly are. Products of the greatest
superpower God has given to us, to share
with the world. Love.

Thank you Daddy, Mama. . . for holding
the ceiling open for us to fly. . .

SOPHIA

Firstly I would like to thank the team at #Merky Books
for such a great opportunity and for being the best
people to work with. A special thank you to: Tallulah
Lyons, Emma Wallace and Lemara Lindsay-Prince —
the time you have all put in to make this book possible
is amazing. It has been great to be part of a project
with such hard-working and friendly people.

I also want to say a big thank you to Dapo Adeola who
has provided so much of his time to help me better
myself as an illustrator; he has been a huge influence
on how I'll approach illustrations moving forward. I
first came across Dapo's work during my second year
at university and I've had the privilege to learn from
him as well as have his genuine support as a mentor.

I've been lucky to have been surrounded by family
and friends that have shown support throughout
the years that I've been pursuing my passion
— I'll always be grateful.

A special thank you to my parents and sisters Aliyah
and Mayah Dankwah who always remind me to keep
going and to never doubt myself. There were times
when I wasn't sure if I made the right choice but
thanks to them and the team at #Merky Books, I
know I'm heading in the right direction.

DENZELL